M ARIAN GETZ SPENT HER CHILDHOOD AS THE DAUGHTER OF MISSIONARIES IN THE CONGO, AFRICA. SHE LEARNED HOW TO COOK BY READING HER MOTHER'S COOKBOOKS AND USING A CAST IRON WOOD BURNING STOVE. SHE OWNED HER OWN CATERING COMPANY IN KANSAS BEFORE BECOMING THE DISTRICT TRAINER FOR CAKE DECORATORS OF A MAJOR FLORIDA GROCERY STORE. A PASTRY CHEF FOR WOLFGANG PUCK SINCE 1998, MARIAN HAS BEEN FEATURED IN SEVERAL NATIONAL MAGAZINES AND WAS SELECTED BY HER PEERS AS ONE OF THE TOP 10 CHEFS IN CENTRAL FLORIDA. SHE HAS ALSO BEEN HONORED WITH THE "OUTSTANDING ACHIEVEMENT AWARD" IN 2007 FROM HER ALMA MATER, OTTAWA UNIVERSITY. MARIAN HAS TAKEN HER EXPERIENCE AS A PASTRY CHEF, WIFE, MOTHER, AND NOW GRANDMOTHER TO PUT TOGETHER A PREP & GARNISH SET COOKBOOK THAT WILL NOT ONLY HELP YOU PREPARE YOUR MEALS FASTER, BUT ALSO LET YOUR CREATE MEMORABLE GARNISHES AND FRUIT DISPLAYS. THIS COLLECTION OF AMAZING RECIPES, MOUTH WATERING PHOTOS, MARIAN'S STEP-BY-STEP TIPS AND RESOURCE PAGE WILL HELP YOU MAKE DELICIOUS FOOD AND INTRICATE FRUIT DISPLAYS FOR ANY OCCASION.

Copyright © 2012 Marian Getz

www.cookbookdesigner.com   Printed in the U.S.A.

ACKNOWLEDGMENTS

A most sincere thank you to our wonderful viewers and customers for without you there would be no need for a cookbook. I try very hard to give you an array of recipes suited for the particular kitchen tool the cookbook is written for. Wolfgang and I create recipes faster than we can write them down. That is what chefs do and is also the reason to tune in to the live shows and even record them so you can learn new dishes that may not be in our cookbooks yet.

Thank you most of all to Wolfgang. You are the most passionate chef I know and it has been a privilege to work for you since 1998. You are a great leader and friend. Your restaurants are full of cooks and staff that have been with you for 20 or more years which is a true testament to how you lead us. Thanks for allowing me to write these cookbooks and for letting me share the stage at HSN with you.

To Greg, my sweet husband since 1983. Working together is a dream and I love you. You have taught me what a treasure it is to have a home filled with people to laugh with.

To my sons, Jordan and Ben, we have a beautiful life, don't we? It just keeps on getting better since we added Lindsay, J. J. and now precious Easton, our first grandbaby.

To all the great people at WP Productions, Syd, Arnie, Mike, Phoebe, Michael, Nicolle, Tracy, Genevieve, Gina, Craig, Nancy, Sylvain, Rodney, Brandon and the rest of the team, you are all amazing to work with. Watching all the wonderful items we sell develop from idea to final product on live television is an awe-inspiring process to see and I love that I get to be a part of it.

To Daniel Koren, our patient editor and photographer, thank you for your dedication. You make the photo shoot days fun and you are such an easygoing person to work with in the cramped, hot studio we have to share. We have learned so much together and have far more to learn.

To Greg, Cat, Estela, Jimmy, Angi, Laurie and Tomasa who are the most dedicated, loving staff anyone could wish for. You are the true heroes behind the scenes. You are a well-oiled machine of very hard working people who pull off the live shows at HSN. It is a magical production to watch, from the first box unpacked, to the thousands of eggs cracked and beaten to running to get that "thing" Wolf asks for at the last minute, to the very last dish washed and put away it is quite a sight to behold. I love you all and I deeply love what we do.

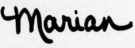

2

It is often said that you eat with your eyes first. Whether in my restaurants or at home, I believe that food presentation is a big part of how we experience our meals. The garnishing set will empower you to be more adventurous in the kitchen. Not only will you be able to prepare your food quicker, but also give it a decorative touch that will turn a great dish into an extraordinary experience.

When I asked Marian to write the cookbook for the garnishing set, I knew she would rise to the occasion. Her experience as a pastry chef, wife, mother, and now a grandmother allowed Marian to put together a garnishing cookbook with a wide variety of recipes that I'm sure you will use for years to come.

A student of cooking is probably one of the best ways to describe Marian. She is always looking for something new, something fresh, something local, something seasonal. Her culinary knowledge combined with her passion for cooking is second to none. The recipes that Marian has written for this cookbook will motivate you to be more creative in the kitchen.

As I learned long ago, alongside my mother and grandmother, you should always put lots of love into everything you cook. This is certainly evident in this cookbook.

Wolfgang Puck

3

FRUIT DISPLAYS

TABLE OF CONTENTS

PREP & GARNISH

Here is a list of my favorite garnishing tools and how I use them everyday for food prep as well as to create memorable fruit displays.

DUAL MELON BALLER

Use the rounded smooth side to scoop perfect balls from a variety of melons, peaches, mango, cheeses and avocado. Use the serrated side to effortlessly remove the core from tomatoes and strawberries.

DUAL CITRUS ZESTER/CHANNEL KNIFE

Use the scalloped end to remove fine curls of zest from a variety of citrus fruits for cooking and garnishing, mixed drinks or lemonade. Use the Channel Knife to make decorative strands of citrus, squashes or melons. It is also great to make a decorative pattern on cucumbers before slicing or use on squashes and melons.

To make long decorative citrus strands for mixed drinks, coil the strands onto a drinking straw or chopstick then secure the ends with a bit of tape. Chill then add to the drink right before serving, the strands will look like a perfect spring.

BIRDS BEAK GARNISHING KNIFE

This thin and curved knife can be used for a variety of tasks such as peeling, carving, slicing and general use in the kitchen. It is also a great tool to devein shrimp by cutting a slit down the outside curve of the shrimp before removing the dark vein with the tip of the knife.

STAINLESS STEEL CHOPPER

Use the sharp blade end to slice, chop and dice ingredients such as vegetables, herbs, cheeses, meats and nuts. The flat side can be used for smashing whole garlic cloves to easily remove the skins. Also use the flat side to scoop and transfer the chopped ingredients into the desired cooking vessel. I often use it to cut bread dough before shaping them into dinner rolls, pizza or cinnamon rolls. It is also great for removing stuck on foods from counters, cutting boards or cookie sheets. I also use it to smooth the sides of a cake with icing for a flawless finish.

CRINKLE CUTTER

Use this cutter to make a decorative crinkle pattern into anything you slice. Use it on vegetables, fruits and cheeses. Great for making crinkle cut French fries and potato chips as well as beautiful vegetable trays. You can also cut doughs, biscuits, brownies and finger sandwiches into pretty shapes.

V-SHAPED CUTTER

Effortlessly cut decorative patterns into melons, squash, cantaloupe and other fruits and vegetables. Adjust the angle of the cutter to change the pattern. It is great for cutting the openings into the different types of watermelon baskets for the fruit displays towards the back of the book.

Y-PEELER

Great for removing skin from a variety of fruits and vegetables such as butternut squash, potatoes, carrots, cucumbers, apples and pears. Also use it to shave fresh Parmesan cheese or chocolate.

PASTRY WHEEL

Use to cut pizza, pie dough, fondant, apple dumplings and bread sticks.

FINE GRATER

Use this tool to grate hard cheeses, garlic cloves, pieces of ginger, chocolate and spices such as cinnamon sticks and whole nutmeg.

PANTRY TIPS

Being prepared to cook the recipes in this book, or any recipe for that matter, is one of the keys to success in the kitchen. Your pantry must be stocked with the basics. We all know how frustrating it can be when you go to the cupboard and what you need is not there. This list includes some of the ingredients you will find in this book and some that we feel are important to always have on hand.

PERISHABLES:

Onions
Garlic
Tomatoes
Carrots
Celery
Ginger
Bell Peppers
White Potatoes
Sweet Potatoes
Squashes
Citrus
Apples
Bananas
Lettuce
Spinach
Fresh Herbs
Green Onions
Milk
Cream Cheese
Parmesan Cheese
Yogurt
Other Cheeses You Like

SPICES:

Kosher Salt
Pepper
Bay Leaves
Sage
Oregano
Thyme
Chili Flakes
Cumin Seeds
Curry Powder
Onion Powder
Garlic Powder
Dry Mustard
Ground Cinnamon
Nutmeg
Cloves
Chili Powder

DRY GOODS:

Sugars
Sugar Substitute
Vanilla
Extracts/Flavorings
Agave Syrup
Canned Tomatoes
Canned Beans
Canned Vegetables
Dried Chilies
Pasta
Lentils
Stocks
Powdered Bouillon
Olives
Ketchup
Mustard
Pickles
Oils
Vinegar
Honey

It is not necessary to have all the items listed at all times. However, if you are feeling creative, adventurous or just following a recipe, it's great to have a good selection in the kitchen.

BBQ BEEF BRISKET DINNER

Makes 6-8 servings

Ingredients:

2 large carrots

2 celery stalks

2 large yellow onions

3 pounds beef brisket, trimmed

1 tablespoon beef bouillon powder, such as Maggi

1 1/2 cups ginger ale or water

1/2 cup ketchup

1 cup BBQ sauce

Kosher salt and fresh black pepper to taste

Method:

1. *Preheat oven to 300°F.*
2. *Use the **Y-PEELER** to peel the carrots then chop carrots and celery using the **CRINKLE CUTTER**.*
3. *Use the **BIRDS BEAK GARNISHING KNIFE** to peel the onions then quarter them using the **STAINLESS STEEL CHOPPER**.*
4. *Use the **STAINLESS STEEL CHOPPER** to gather up the carrots and onions; transfer to a large Dutch oven.*
5. *Layer remaining ingredients in the Dutch oven in the order listed; cover with lid.*
6. *Bake for 4 hours or until meat is tender.*
7. *When baking is complete, garnish as desired before serving.*

TIP

This recipe can also be made in a slow cooker (follow manufacturer instructions).

EASY GLAZED MEATLOAF

Makes 4-6 servings

For the Meatloaf:

3 white bread slices
1 large yellow onion
2 garlic cloves
4 bacon slices
1/3 cup whole milk
1 pound lean ground beef
1/2 pound ground pork
2 large eggs, beaten
1 teaspoon kosher salt
1/2 teaspoon freshly cracked pepper
1/3 cup ketchup
1 tablespoon yellow mustard
1 tablespoon Worcestershire sauce
Parsley for garnish

For the Glaze:

1/4 cup yellow mustard
1/3 cup ketchup
1 cup light brown sugar, packed

Method:

1. *Preheat oven to 350°F.*
2. *Use the **KITCHEN SHEARS** to cut the bread into cubes.*
3. *Use the **BIRDS BEAK GARNISHING KNIFE** to peel the onion then finely chop it using the **STAINLESS STEEL CHOPPER**.*
4. *Use the **STAINLESS STEEL CHOPPER** to smash and chop the garlic.*
5. *Use the **CRINKLE CUTTER** to finely chop the bacon.*
6. *In a bowl, combine the bread cubes and milk; let stand for 5 minutes.*
7. *Add remaining meatloaf ingredients, except parsley, to the bowl; mix gently together.*
8. *Apply nonstick spray to a baking pan or bread pan.*
9. *Press the meatloaf mixture into the pan then smooth the top; cover with aluminum foil.*
10. *Place pan in oven and bake for 1 hour.*
11. *Combine all glaze ingredients in a saucepan over medium heat.*
12. *Simmer for 5 minutes or until thick and shiny.*
13. *When baking is complete, remove meatloaf from the oven and top with glaze.*
14. *Use the **KITCHEN SHEARS** to cut parsley over the meatloaf before serving.*

RECIPES

CHEESY BURGER
MAC

Makes 4 servings

Ingredients:

1 small yellow onion

1 tablespoon unsalted butter

1 tablespoon tomato paste

8 ounces ground beef

Kosher salt and fresh pepper to taste

6-ounce block sharp Cheddar cheese

4-ounce block mozzarella cheese

3/4 cup milk

8 ounces pasta, cooked

Green onions

Method:

1. Use the **BIRDS BEAK GARNISHING KNIFE** to peel the onion then chop it using the **CRINKLE CUTTER.**

2. Preheat a saucepan over medium heat.

3. Melt the butter in the pan.

4. Use the **STAINLESS STEEL CHOPPER** to scoop and transfer the onions to the pan; cook for 5 minutes or until softened, stirring often.

5. Add the tomato paste to the pan; stir.

6. Add the ground beef and cook for 4-5 minutes or until browned.

7. Season to taste with salt and pepper.

8. Use the **FINE GRATER** to grate both cheeses.

9. Add the milk and cheese to the pan; stir until cheese is melted (reserve 2 ounces of Cheddar cheese for topping).

10. Add the pasta and gently stir to combine.

11. Top with reserved Cheddar cheese; cover with lid.

12. Reduce heat to low and cook until cheese is melted.

13. Use the **KITCHEN SHEARS** to snip the green onions for garnish before serving.

EASY ONE SKILLET
BEEF STROGANOFF

Makes 4 servings

Ingredients:

1 1/2 pounds sirloin beef

Kosher salt and fresh pepper to taste

2 tablespoons olive oil

2 large yellow onions

2 garlic cloves

2 packages (10 ounces) button mushrooms

3 cups beef stock

2 teaspoons soy sauce

3 tablespoons brandy or Madeira

3 cups dry egg noodles

2/3 cup sour cream

Fresh parsley

Method:

1. Use the **BIRDS BEAK GARNISHING KNIFE** to slice the beef into thin strips then season with salt and pepper.
2. Preheat the oil in a large skillet over medium-high heat.
3. When oil is hot, add the beef to the skillet; sear on all sides.
4. While meat is searing, use the **BIRDS BEAK GARNISHING KNIFE** to peel the onions then slice using the **CRINKLE CUTTER** and add to the skillet.
5. Use the **STAINLESS STEEL CHOPPER** to smash and chop the garlic then scoop and transfer to the skillet.
6. Use the **CRINKLE CUTTER** to slice the mushrooms then add to the skillet.
7. Add the stock and soy sauce to the skillet; stir thoroughly, scraping the bottom of the skillet.
8. Add the brandy to the skillet; cover then reduce heat to a simmer.
9. Cook for 20 minutes or just until beef is almost tender.
10. Stir in the noodles, cover then cook for an additional 8 minutes.
11. When cooking is complete, remove from heat then stir in the sour cream.
12. Use the **KITCHEN SHEARS** to snip parsley over the dish, garnish as desired and serve.

EASY ONE SKILLET
BAKED SPAGHETTI

Makes 4-6 servings

Ingredients:

2 teaspoons olive oil
1 pound Italian sausage
1 large yellow onion
6 garlic cloves
2 teaspoons Italian seasoning
1 can (28 ounces) diced tomatoes
Kosher salt and fresh pepper to taste
2 cups hot beef stock
8 ounces dried spaghetti, broken
A small wedge of Parmesan cheese
2-ounce block mozzarella cheese
Fresh basil leaves
Fresh chives

Method:

1. *Preheat the oil in a large skillet over medium-high heat.*
2. *Use the **KITCHEN SHEARS** to remove casings from the sausage.*
3. *Use the **STAINLESS STEEL CHOPPER** to roughly chop the Italian sausage.*
4. *Use the **STAINLESS STEEL CHOPPER** to scoop and transfer the sausage to the skillet.*
5. *Use the **BIRDS BEAK GARNISHING KNIFE** to peel the onion.*
6. *Use the **STAINLESS STEEL CHOPPER** to coarsely chop the onion then scoop and transfer to the skillet.*
7. *Use the **STAINLESS STEEL CHOPPER** to smash and chop the garlic then scoop and transfer to the skillet.*
8. *When sausage is no longer pink, add the Italian seasoning, tomatoes, salt and pepper; stir.*
9. *Add the hot stock and spaghetti; cover then turn heat to medium-low and cook for 6 minutes.*
10. *Remove the lid, stir, then cover again and cook for an additional 6 minutes.*
11. *Stir, test noodles for doneness and remove from heat when done.*
12. *Use the **FINE GRATER** to grate both cheeses over the spaghetti.*
13. *If desired place under the broiler for 2-3 minutes or until lightly browned.*
14. *Use the **KITCHEN SHEARS** to snip basil and chives over the spaghetti before serving.*

SWISS STEAK

Makes 4 servings

Ingredients:

1 large yellow onion
2 large carrots
2 celery stalks
8 very small red skinned potatoes
1 tablespoon canola oil
4 pieces (2 pounds) cube steak

2 tablespoon red wine vinegar
1 cup beef stock
1 bay leaf
3 tablespoons tomato paste
Kosher salt and fresh pepper to taste
Green onions

Method:

1. Use the **BIRDS BEAK GARNISHING KNIFE** to peel the onion then chop it using the **STAINLESS STEEL CHOPPER**.
2. Use the **Y-PEELER** to peel the carrots.
3. Use the **CRINKLE CUTTER** to slice the carrots and celery.
4. Use **BIRDS BEAK GARNISHING KNIFE** to cut the potatoes in half.
5. Preheat the oil in a large sauté pan over medium-high heat.
6. When oil is hot, add the steak pieces to the pan; brown lightly on both sides.
7. Place remaining ingredients, except green onions, to the pan; cover with lid.
8. Reduce heat to low and simmer for 40 minutes or until meat is tender.
9. Taste and adjust seasoning if desired.
10. Use the **KITCHEN SHEARS** to snip green onions for garnish before serving.

14

CHILI CON CARNE

Makes 4-6 servings

Ingredients:

1 large white onion
6 garlic cloves
1/4 cup green onions
2 pounds beef brisket, trimmed
4 bacon slices
4 tablespoons chili powder
1 tablespoon ground cumin seeds
1 tablespoon oregano leaves
Kosher salt and fresh pepper to taste
4 cups water
2 cups canned tomato puree
1 teaspoon honey
Juice from 1 lime
1 jalapeño pepper, diced (optional)
3 cans (15.5 ounces each) dark red kidney beans

Method:

1. *Preheat a large stockpot over medium heat.*
2. *Use the **BIRDS BEAK GARNISHING KNIFE** to peel the onion then chop it using the **STAINLESS STEEL CHOPPER.***
3. *Use the **STAINLESS STEEL CHOPPER** to smash and chop the garlic.*
4. *Use the **KITCHEN SHEARS** to snip the green onions.*
5. *Use the **CRINKLE CUTTER** to cut the brisket into 1-inch cubes.*
6. *Use the **STAINLESS STEEL CHOPPER** to dice the bacon then scoop and transfer to the stockpot.*
7. *Cook bacon until most of the fat has rendered out of it then remove the bacon and set aside.*
8. *Add 1 pound of beef to the stockpot; brown lightly on all sides then remove from stockpot.*
9. *Repeat with remaining beef.*
10. *Place all of the beef, bacon and remaining ingredients in the stockpot; cover, reduce heat to low and cook for 1 hour.*
11. *Taste and adjust seasoning if desired.*
12. *Garnish as desired and serve.*

HEARTY BEEF
STEW

Makes 4-6 servings

Ingredients:

2 large yellow onions
2 garlic cloves
3 Russet potatoes
3 carrots
2 celery stalks
1 pound beef chuck
2 tablespoons canola oil
2 tablespoons cornstarch
Kosher salt and fresh pepper to taste
6 cups beef stock
1/4 cup ketchup
1 tablespoon Worcestershire sauce
2 teaspoons soy sauce
1 bay leaf

Method:

1. *Use the **BIRDS BEAK GARNISHING KNIFE** to peel the onions then chop it using the **STAINLESS STEEL CHOPPER**.*
2. *Use the **STAINLESS STEEL CHOPPER** to smash and chop the garlic.*
3. *Use the **Y-PEELER** to peel the potatoes then cube them using the **BIRDS BEAK GARNISHING KNIFE**.*
4. *Use the **Y-PEELER** to peel the carrots then cut carrots and celery into chunks using the **CRINKLE CUTTER**.*
5. *Use the **CRINKLE CUTTER** to cut beef into 1-inch cubes.*
6. *Preheat the oil in a large stockpot over medium-high heat.*
7. *Sprinkle the cornstarch, salt and pepper evenly over the beef.*
8. *Add the beef to the stockpot in batches and brown on all sides.*
9. *Add remaining ingredients and all of the beef to the stockpot; cover with lid.*
10. *Reduce heat to low and cook for 1 - 1 1/2 hours or until meat is tender.*
11. *When cooking is complete, adjust seasoning if desired before serving.*

BEEF & NOODLES

Makes 4-6 servings

Ingredients:

1/2 medium yellow onion
2 celery stalks
4 ounces button mushrooms
2 garlic cloves
1 tablespoon unsalted butter
1 pound ground beef
1/2 cup chicken stock
1 cup evaporated milk
Kosher salt and fresh pepper to taste
Green onions for garnish
Hot buttered noodles, cooked
Sour Cream (optional)

Method:

1. *Preheat a sauté pan over medium-high heat.*
2. *Use the **BIRDS BEAK GARNISHING KNIFE** to peel the onion then use the **CRINKLE CUTTER** to chop the onions, celery and mushrooms; set aside.*
3. *Use the **STAINLESS STEEL CHOPPER** to smash and chop the garlic; set aside.*
4. *Melt the butter in the pan.*
5. *Add the ground beef to the pan; stir and cook until no pink remains.*
6. *Use the **STAINLESS STEEL CHOPPER** to scoop and transfer the onions, celery, mushrooms and garlic to the pan; cook for 3 minutes or until onions are tender.*
7. *Add remaining ingredients, except green onions, noodles and sour cream; cover with lid.*
8. *Cook for 10-12 minutes then taste and adjust seasoning if desired.*
9. *Use the **KITCHEN SHEARS** to snip the green onions for garnishing.*
10. *Serve over buttered noodles garnished with a dollop of sour cream if desired and green onions.*

EASY SKILLET
LASAGNA

Makes 4-6 servings

Ingredients:

1 large yellow onion
3 garlic cloves
1 tablespoon canola oil
2 teaspoons Italian seasoning
1 pound ground beef
Kosher salt and fresh pepper to taste
10 lasagna noodles, broken up
1 can (28 ounces) diced tomatoes
1 can (8 ounces) tomato sauce
1 cup water
2-ounce wedge Parmesan cheese
1 cup ricotta cheese

Method:

1. *Use the **BIRDS BEAK GARNISHING KNIFE** to peel the onion then chop it using the **CRINKLE CUTTER**.*
2. *Use the **STAINLESS STEEL CHOPPER** to smash and chop the garlic.*
3. *Preheat the oil in a large skillet over medium heat.*
4. *Add the onions to the skillet and cook for 5 minutes or until onions start to brown.*
5. *Add the garlic and Italian seasoning; cook for 1 minute.*
6. *Add the ground beef, season with salt and pepper then cook for 5 minutes or until beef is done.*
7. *Scatter the noodles over the beef; do not stir.*
8. *Pour the tomatoes, tomato sauce and water over the noodles; cover and bring to a simmer.*
9. *Reduce heat to low and cook for 10 minutes, stirring occasionally, or until noodles are tender.*
10. *While cooking, use the **FINE GRATER** to grate the Parmesan cheese.*
11. *When cooking is complete, remove from heat then top lasagna with both cheeses.*
12. *Garnish as desired before serving.*

RECIPES

MEXICAN BEEF CASSEROLE

Makes 4-6 servings

For the Casserole:

1 large yellow onion
1 jalapeño pepper
1 tablespoon canola oil
1 pound ground beef
1 can (15.5 ounces) kidney beans, drained and rinsed
1 can (15.5 ounces) yellow corn
1 jar (17.35 ounces) enchilada sauce
1 can (4 ounces) diced green chiles
1 package (1.12 ounces) taco seasoning mix
2 cups beef stock

For Serving:

4 cups tortilla chips
1 cup Monterrey Jack cheese
Jalapeño peppers
Sour cream
Green onions

Method:

1. *Preheat oven to 350°F.*
2. *Use the **BIRDS BEAK GARNISHING KNIFE** to peel the onion then chop the onion and jalapeño pepper using the **CRINKLE CUTTER**.*
3. *Preheat the oil in a large skillet over medium-high heat.*
4. *When oil is hot, add the beef; cook and stir until no longer pink then transfer to a 9 x 13-inch baking dish.*
5. *Add remaining casserole ingredients to the baking dish; stir well.*
6. *Bake for 30-40 minutes or until brown and bubbly.*
7. *Add the tortilla chips to the casserole.*
8. *Use the **FINE GRATER** to shred the cheese over the casserole then serve as desired.*

CHEESEBURGER
PIZZA

Makes 1 pizza

Ingredients:

1 tablespoon canola oil
1 pound ground beef
Kosher salt and fresh pepper to taste
1 medium yellow onion
1 pound pizza dough, store-bought

1/2 cup ketchup
1/4 cup yellow mustard
2 dill pickles
1 small wedge Cheddar cheese

Method:

1. *Preheat oven to 450°F.*
2. *Preheat the oil in a large sauté pan over medium-high heat.*
3. *When pan is hot, add the ground beef; seasoning with salt and pepper.*
4. *While beef is browning, use the **BIRDS BEAK GARNISHING KNIFE** to peel the onion.*
5. *Use the **FINE GRATER** to grate the onion over the ground beef in the pan; stir.*
6. *When meat is browned, remove and drain.*
7. *Pat out the pizza dough on a greased jelly roll pan.*
8. *In a small bowl, stir together the ketchup and mustard.*
9. *Spread the ketchup mixture over the dough then top with the ground beef mixture.*
10. *Use the **Y-PEELER** to thinly shave the pickles; scatter over the pizza.*
11. *Use the **FINE GRATER** to shred the cheese over the pizza until evenly covered.*
12. *Bake for 20 minutes or until browned and bubbly then remove and let stand for 5 minutes.*
13. *Use the **PASTRY WHEEL** to cut pizza into slices then use the **STAINLESS STEEL CHOPPER** to lift and serve the slices.*

BEEF BRISKET &
VEGGIES

Makes 6-8 servings

Ingredients:

4 pounds beef brisket, trimmed

1 tablespoon kosher salt

1 teaspoon freshly cracked black pepper

1 tablespoon olive oil

4 large carrots

4 parsnips

2 large yellow onions

10 garlic cloves

3 celery stalks

4 fresh sage leaves

4 bay leaves

1 cup very strong beef stock

1/2 cup ketchup

2 tablespoons soy sauce

1/2 cup dry red wine

Method:

1. *Preheat oven to 325°F and preheat a large Dutch oven on a stove over medium-high heat.*

2. *Pat the brisket dry using paper towels then season with salt and pepper.*

3. *Add the oil to the Dutch oven.*

4. *When oil is hot, add the brisket; sear on both sides until well browned then remove from heat.*

5. *Use the **Y-PEELER** to peel the carrots and parsnips then use the **CRINKLE CUTTER** to cut both into chunks.*

6. *Use the **STAINLESS STEEL CHOPPER** to scoop and transfer the carrots and parsnips to the Dutch oven.*

7. *Use the **BIRDS BEAK GARNISHING KNIFE** to peel the onions; chop onions using the **CRINKLE CUTTER** then scoop and transfer to the Dutch oven using the **STAINLESS STEEL CHOPPER.***

8. *Use the **STAINLESS STEEL CHOPPER** to smash and chop the garlic then scoop and transfer to the Dutch oven.*

9. *Use the **CRINKLE CUTTER** to roughly chop the celery; transfer to the Dutch oven.*

10. *Use the **KITCHEN SHEARS** to snip sage leaves into the Dutch oven then add the bay leaves.*

11. *In a bowl, whisk together the stock, ketchup, soy sauce and wine.*

12. *Pour wine mixture into the Dutch oven; stir well then cover and place in the oven.*

13. *Cook in the oven for 4 hours or until brisket is very tender.*

14. *When cooking is complete, skim off any excess fat then slice the brisket.*

15. *Garnish as desired then serve brisket and vegetables with some of the juices.*

SPAGHETTI & MEATBALLS

Makes 4-6 servings

For the Sauce:

2 garlic cloves
1 large carrot
4 tablespoons good quality Italian olive oil
1 can (28 ounces) crushed tomatoes
1 can (10 ounces) tomato puree
Kosher salt and fresh pepper to taste

For the Meatballs:

1 pound ground sirloin
1/4 pound ground pork
5 sprigs flat leaf parsley
2-ounce block Parmesan cheese
2 large garlic coves, minced
3 large eggs
1 tablespoon kosher salt
1/2 teaspoon fresh pepper
4 Italian bread slices, soaked in 1/2 cup water
3 tablespoons good quality Italian olive oil
Cooked pasta for serving

Method:

1. Use the **STAINLESS STEEL CHOPPER** to smash and chop the garlic.
2. Use the **Y-PEELER** to peel the carrot.
3. Heat the oil in a stockpot over medium heat.
4. When oil is hot, add the garlic and stir until fragrant.
5. Add the crushed tomatoes and tomato puree; bring to a gentle simmer.
6. Add the carrot and simmer for 30 minutes; taste and adjust seasoning if desired.
7. While sauce is simmering, combine the sirloin and pork in a bowl.
8. Use the **KITCHEN SHEARS** to snip the parsley.
9. Use the **FINE GRATER** to grate the Parmesan cheese.
10. Add the garlic, cheese, parsley, eggs, salt, pepper and soaked bread to the bowl.
11. Mix using your hands and then form mixture into 1 1/2-inch balls.
12. Heat the oil in a sauté pan over medium heat.
13. When oil is hot, add the meatballs in batches and brown them well until cooked through.
14. Add cooked meatballs to the sauce and simmer for an additional 30 minutes.
15. When cooking is complete, discard carrot, garnish as desire and serve over pasta.

SKILLET
TAMALE PIE

Makes 6-8 servings

Ingredients:

1 pound ground beef or turkey
2 large yellow onions
4 garlic cloves
1-2 jalapeño peppers
1 can (7 ounces) mild green chiles
3 tablespoons chili powder
1 teaspoon ground cumin
1 can (14.5 ounces) diced tomatoes
Kosher salt and fresh pepper to taste
3 1/2 cups chicken stock
1 cup yellow cornmeal
6-ounce block Monterey Jack cheese
3 cups frozen yellow corn, thawed
Fresh cilantro

Method:

1. *Preheat a large skillet over medium-high heat.*
2. *Add the beef to the skillet; break up the meat while browning.*
3. *Use the **BIRDS BEAK GARNISHING KNIFE** to peel the onions then chop them using the **CRINKLE CUTTER**; add to the skillet.*
4. *Use the **STAINLESS STEEL CHOPPER** to smash and chop the garlic.*
5. *Use the **BIRDS BEAK GARNISHING KNIFE** to slice the jalapeño peppers; add garlic and jalapeño to the skillet.*
6. *Stir and cook until beef is no longer pink then add the chiles, chili powder, cumin and tomatoes; season with salt and pepper and stir.*
7. *In a large saucepan, bring the chicken stock to a boil over medium-high heat.*
8. *Add the cornmeal and whisk constantly for 2-3 minutes or until thick and bubbly; remove.*
9. *Use the **FINE GRATER** to grate the cheese then add half to cornmeal mixture along with the corn to the saucepan; stir, season with salt and pepper then remove from heat.*
10. *Pour the cornmeal mixture evenly over the beef mixture then top with remaining cheese.*
11. *Preheat a broiler then broil for 5 minutes or until brown, bubbly and cheese has all melted.*
12. *Use the **KITCHEN SHEARS** to snip cilantro for garnish before serving.*

EASY CHICKEN
POT PIE

Makes 6 servings

Ingredients:

1 tablespoon canola oil
6 boneless, skinless chicken breasts or thighs
Kosher salt and fresh pepper to taste
1 large yellow onion
3 large carrots
3 celery stalks
3 bay leaves
2 cups chicken stock
1/2 cup half & half
1/4 cup all purpose flour
1/2 cup whole milk
1 tube refrigerator biscuits, baked

Method:

1. *Preheat the oil in a large skillet over medium-high heat.*
2. *Season chicken with salt and pepper then place in the skillet; brown on all sides.*
3. *Use the **BIRDS BEAK GARNISHING KNIFE** to peel the onion then use the **CRINKLE CUTTER** to chop it.*
4. *Use the **STAINLESS STEEL CHOPPER** to scoop and transfer the onions over the chicken.*
5. *Use the **Y-PEELER** to peel the carrots; chop the carrots and celery using the **CRINKLE CUTTER**.*
6. *Use the **STAINLESS STEEL CHOPPER** to scoop and transfer carrots and celery to the skillet.*
7. *Stir ingredients then add the bay leaves, stock, half & half; season to taste with salt and pepper.*
8. *Let simmer for 15 minutes.*
9. *In a bowl, combine flour and milk then whisk flour mixture into the bubbling chicken mixture to thicken.*
10. *Top with biscuits before serving.*

BEST PAN
ROASTED CHICKEN

Makes 4 servings

Ingredients:

1 whole chicken, cut into 8 pieces
1 large yellow onion
1 pound red bliss potatoes
8 fresh thyme sprigs
8 fresh sage leaves

3 tablespoons olive oil
1 tablespoon unsalted butter, melted
Kosher salt and fresh pepper to taste
1 lemon

Method:

1. *Preheat oven to 400°F.*
2. *Use the **CRINKLE CUTTER** and **KITCHEN SHEARS** to cut chicken into 8 pieces then place on a 1/2-sheet pan.*
3. *Use the **BIRDS BEAK GARNISHING KNIFE** to peel the onion then chop is using the **CRINKLE CUTTER**.*
4. *Use the **STAINLESS STEEL CHOPPER** to scoop and transfer the onions to the 1/2-sheet pan.*
5. *Use the **BIRDS BEAK GARNISHING KNIFE** to cut the potatoes in half.*
6. *Use the **STAINLESS STEEL CHOPPER** to scoop and transfer the potatoes to the 1/2 sheet pan.*
7. *Use the **KITCHEN SHEARS** to snip the thyme and sage over the chicken.*
8. *Drizzle with the oil and butter then season liberally with salt and pepper.*
9. *Use the **FINE GRATER** to zest the lemon over the chicken.*
10. *Use the **BIRDS BEAK GARNISHING KNIFE** to cut the lemon in half; squeeze lemon juice over the ingredients on the 1/2-sheet pan then toss well.*
11. *Arrange all ingredients in a single layer on the 1/2-sheet pan.*
12. *Bake for 35 minutes or until food is well browned and chicken reaches 165°F on a meat thermometer.*

RASPBERRY GLAZED CHICKEN

Makes 4 servings

Ingredients:

1 large yellow onion
1 tablespoon unsalted butter
4 boneless, skinless chicken breasts
Kosher salt and fresh pepper to taste
1 yellow bell pepper
1 garlic clove
1/2 cup red wine
1/4 cup raspberry vinegar
2 tablespoons raspberry jam
1/4 cup soy sauce
2 tablespoons honey
1 teaspoon Dijon mustard
1 bunch green onions

Method:

1. *Use the **BIRDS BEAK GARNISHING KNIFE** to peel the onion then julienne it using the **CRINKLE CUTTER.***

2. *Melt the butter in a large skillet over medium-high heat.*

3. *Add the onions to the skillet.*

4. *Use the **BIRDS BEAK GARNISHING KNIFE** to trim the chicken then add to the skillet.*

5. *Season chicken with salt and pepper then brown on both sides.*

6. *Use the **CRINKLE CUTTER** to julienne the bell pepper then add to the skillet.*

7. *Use the **STAINLESS STEEL CHOPPER** to smash and chop the garlic then add to the skillet.*

8. *Add the wine, vinegar, jam, soy sauce, honey and mustard to the skillet; bring to a simmer and cook until the chicken is just cooked through.*

9. *Remove from heat then use the **KITCHEN SHEARS** to snip green onions over the dish before serving.*

EASY CHICKEN
TACOS

Makes 4 servings

Ingredients:

1/4 wedge iceberg lettuce

1 large red onion

2 Roma tomatoes

1 carrot

1 jalapeño pepper

12 ounces rotisserie chicken, bones removed

4-ounce block Cheddar cheese

8 taco shells

Salsa (optional)

Method:

1. Use the **CRINKLE CUTTER** to chop and shred the lettuce.
2. Use the **BIRDS BEAK GARNISHING KNIFE** to peel and slice the onion.
3. Use the **DUAL MELON BALLER** to core tomatoes then chop using the **STAINLESS STEEL CHOPPER**.
4. Use the **Y-PEELER** to peel the carrot then grate it using the **FINE GRATER**.
5. Use the **BIRDS BEAK GARNISHING KNIFE** to seed and slice the jalapeño pepper and slice the chicken.
6. Use the **FINE GRATER** to grate the cheese.
7. Place ingredients into the taco shell then top with cheese and salsa if desired before serving.

QUICK & EASY
CHICKEN DIVAN

Makes 4 servings

Ingredients:

2 tablespoons canola oil, divided
4 boneless, skinless chicken breasts
Kosher salt and fresh pepper to taste
1/2 cup all purpose flour
1 large yellow onion
1 cup strong chicken stock
3/4 cup heavy cream
3-ounce block of Parmesan cheese
2 teaspoons Worcestershire sauce
2 tablespoons brandy
1 tablespoon lemon juice
1 bag (16 ounces) frozen broccoli florets

Method:

1. *Preheat 1 tablespoon oil in a large skillet over medium heat.*
2. *Use the **KITCHEN SHEARS** to trim any fat from chicken breasts.*
3. *Season chicken with salt and pepper then sprinkle all sides with flour.*
4. *When oil is hot, place the chicken into the skillet; cook for 5 minutes on each side or until just cooked through.*
5. *Remove chicken to a plate and set aside; add remaining oil to the skillet.*
6. *Use the **BIRDS BEAK GARNISHING KNIFE** to peel the onion then julienne it using the **CRINKLE CUTTER**.*
7. *Add the onions to the skillet and cook for 10 minutes or until browned.*
8. *Add the stock and cream to the skillet; simmer for 5 minutes.*
9. *Use the **FINE GRATER** to grate the Parmesan cheese then add all but 1/3 cup of cheese to the skillet; stir.*
10. *Add the Worcestershire sauce, brandy and lemon juice; adjust seasoning if desired.*
11. *Add the broccoli to the skillet.*
12. *Return the chicken to the skillet and spoon some sauce and broccoli over it.*
13. *Top chicken with the reserved Parmesan cheese; cover and let stand for 5 minutes or until cheese is melted then garnish as desired before serving.*

WHOLE CHICKEN SOUP

Makes 6 servings

Ingredients:

1 whole chicken (3-4 pounds)
1 medium yellow onion
3 sprigs fresh dill
3 sprigs fresh thyme
2 carrots
1 celery stalk
1 large leek, white and light green part only, cleaned
Kosher salt and fresh pepper to taste
Water to cover the chicken
Green onions

Method:

1. Use the **KITCHEN SHEARS** to trim excess skin and fat from the chicken.
2. Use the **BIRDS BEAK GARNISHING KNIFE** to peel the onion then chop it using the **STAINLESS STEEL CHOPPER**.
3. Use the **KITCHEN SHEARS** to snip the dill and thyme.
4. Use the **Y-PEELER** to peel the carrots then cut carrots and celery into 1-inch pieces using the **CRINKLE CUTTER**.
5. Use the **STAINLESS STEEL CHOPPER** to chop the leak.
6. Place all ingredients, except water and green onions, into a large stockpot.
7. Add enough water to just cover the chicken.
8. Place stockpot on the stove over medium heat; cover with lid.
9. Cook for 45 - 60 minutes or until chicken is tender.
10. Use the **KITCHEN SHEARS** to snip green onions for garnish.
11. Use tongs to pull the chicken apart before serving.

CHICKEN CURRY
IN A HURRY

Makes 4-6 servings

Ingredients:

1 medium yellow onion
2 garlic cloves
1-inch piece of ginger
2 tablespoons unsalted butter
2 tablespoons curry powder
1 teaspoon ground turmeric
3 tablespoons Thai red curry paste
6 chicken breasts

2 cups water
1 tablespoon chicken bouillon powder
2 tablespoons cornstarch
1 cup unsweetened coconut milk
1 lime, juice and zest
2 teaspoons honey
Kosher salt to taste
Cooked rice for serving

Method:

1. Use the **BIRDS BEAK GARNISHING KNIFE** to peel the onion then chop it using the **STAINLESS STEEL CHOPPER**.

2. Use the **STAINLESS STEEL CHOPPER** to smash and chop the garlic.

3. Use the **BIRDS BEAK GARNISHING KNIFE** to peel the ginger then grate it using the **FINE GRATER**.

4. Melt the butter in a large Dutch oven over medium-high heat.

5. Add the curry powder and turmeric to the Dutch oven; stir until fragrant.

6. Use the **STAINLESS STEEL CHOPPER** to scoop and transfer the onions, garlic and ginger (reserve 1 tablespoon ginger) to the Dutch oven then add the curry paste; stir.

7. Add the chicken, water and chicken bouillon; cover with lid then reduce heat to low.

8. Simmer for 30-45 minutes or until chicken is tender.

9. Stir the cornstarch into the coconut milk then pour mixture into the Dutch oven; stir until thickened then turn off the heat.

10. Use the **FINE GRATER** to zest the lime.

11. Stir in the remaining ginger, lime zest, juice from the lime and honey.

12. Taste and adjust seasoning if desired.

13. Garnish as desired and serve over rice.

CHICKEN
BOLOGNESE

Makes 6 servings

Ingredients:

1 large yellow onion

1 large carrot

1 stalk celery

1 tablespoon unsalted butter

3 tablespoons tomato paste

1/2 cup water

1 tablespoon olive oil

1 pound ground chicken thighs

Kosher salt and fresh pepper to taste

2 garlic cloves

1/4 cup dry white wine

3 cups chicken stock

1 can (28 ounces) diced tomatoes

1/2 cup whole milk

2 tablespoons heavy cream

1 pound pasta, cooked

Ricotta cheese

Method:

1. Use the **BIRDS BEAK GARNISHING KNIFE** to peel the onion then quarter it using the **STAINLESS STEEL CHOPPER**.

2. Use the **Y-PEELER** to peel the carrot.

3. Use the **STAINLESS STEEL CHOPPER** to cut the carrot and celery into chunks.

4. Use the **STAINLESS STEEL CHOPPER** to scoop and transfer the onions, carrots and celery to a blender; cover and pulse until fine.

5. Melt the butter in a large saucepot over medium heat.

6. Add the onion mixture and cook for about 15 minutes, stirring often, or until vegetables are brown.

7. Add the tomato paste and cook for a few additional minutes until tomato paste is browned.

8. Add the water and stir well to scrape up all the brown bits from the bottom of the pot.

9. Add the olive oil and chicken; season with salt and pepper and cook for 10 minutes.

10. Use the **BIRDS BEAK GARNISHING KNIFE** to peel garlic then chop it using the **STAINLESS STEEL CHOPPER**; add the garlic to the pot and stir until fragrant.

11. Add the wine, stock, tomatoes and milk; stir then adjust seasoning if desired.

12. Cover with lid then turn heat to low and simmer for 2 hours, stirring occasionally.

13. Stir in the cream and adjust seasoning if desired.

14. Serve over pasta topped with ricotta cheese.

EASY CHICKEN
A LA KING

Makes 4 servings

Ingredients:

4 boneless, skinless chicken breasts
1/2 cup heavy cream
2 1/2 teaspoons kosher salt
1 lemon
1 large yellow onion
8 ounces button mushrooms
1 garlic clove
1 red bell pepper
3 tablespoons unsalted butter
3 tablespoons all purpose flour
1/3 cup Madeira wine or brandy
1 cup strong chicken stock
1 cup frozen peas, thawed
8 slices buttered toast

Method:

1. *Use the **KITCHEN SHEARS** to trim any fat from the chicken then dice using the **CRINKLE CUTTER**.*

2. *In a bowl, combine the chicken, cream and salt.*

3. *Use the **CITRUS ZESTER** to zest the lemon over the chicken in the bowl.*

4. *Use the **BIRDS BEAK GARNISHING KNIFE** to cut the lemon in half then squeeze the juice over the chicken; stir and let marinate for 15 minutes.*

5. *Use the **BIRDS BEAK GARNISHING KNIFE** to peel the onion; chop the onion and mushrooms.*

6. *Use the **STAINLESS STEEL CHOPPER** to smash and chop the garlic.*

7. *Use the **BIRDS BEAK GARNISHING KNIFE** to julienne bell pepper.*

8. *Melt the butter in a large skillet over medium heat.*

9. *Add the onions, mushrooms and garlic; sauté for 5 minutes then add the flour; stir until smooth.*

10. *Add remaining ingredients, except toast; stir well then raise heat to medium-high.*

11. *Cook for 8-9 minutes or until chicken is just cooked through and sauce is bubbly.*

12. *Place 2 slices of toast on each serving plate then top with chicken mixture.*

EASY SKILLET CHICKEN
CASSEROLE

Makes 4 servings

Ingredients:

4 cups really good chicken stock
4 boneless, skinless chicken breasts
1 large yellow onion
1 large carrot
1 celery stalk
A few sage leaves
Kosher salt and fresh pepper to taste
2 teaspoons apple cider vinegar
2 cups dry elbow macaroni pasta
1 cup half & half
2 cups panko breadcrumbs
Handful of parsley

Method:

1. Preheat the chicken stock in a large skillet over medium-high heat.
2. Use the **CRINKLE CUTTER** to dice the chicken then use the **STAINLESS STEEL CHOPPER** to scoop and transfer the chicken to the skillet.
3. Use the **BIRDS BEAK GARNISHING KNIFE** to peel onion then chop it using the **CRINKLE CUTTER**.
4. Use the **Y-PEELER** to peel the carrot.
5. Chop the carrot and celery using the **CRINKLE CUTTER** then use the **STAINLESS STEEL CHOPPER** to scoop and transfer into the skillet over the chicken.
6. Use the **KITCHEN SHEARS** to snip the sage leaves over the chicken then season with salt and pepper.
7. Add the vinegar, pasta and half & half to the skillet then bring to a boil; turn heat to low, cover and cook for 5 minutes.
8. Stir well, then cover and cook for an additional 5 minutes or until pasta is just tender.
9. When cooking is complete, remove from heat then preheat the broiler.
10. Top casserole with panko and place under the broiler for 2-3 minutes or until lightly browned.
11. Use the **KITCHEN SHEARS** to snip parsley over the casserole before serving (if you prefer a thicker consistency, let stand for 10 minutes before serving).

ONE SKILLET CHICKEN
VESUVIO

Makes 4 servings

Ingredients:

4 boneless, skinless chicken breasts
Kosher salt and fresh pepper to taste
1 tablespoon olive oil, divided
4 garlic cloves
1 pound small red skinned potatoes
1 sprig fresh rosemary
2 sprigs fresh oregano
1/2 cup white wine
1 cup chicken stock
1 bag (8 ounces) frozen peas
1 lemon

Method:

1. *Use the **KITCHEN SHEARS** to trim excess fat from the chicken; season with salt and pepper.*
2. *Preheat 1/2 tablespoon oil in a large skillet over medium heat.*
3. *When oil is hot, add the chicken to the skillet; brown on each side for 5 minutes.*
4. *While chicken is browning, use the **STAINLESS STEEL CHOPPER** to smash and chop the garlic; set aside.*
5. *Use the **BIRDS BEAK GARNISHING KNIFE** to quarter or half the potatoes.*
6. *Remove chicken to a plate then add remaining oil to the skillet.*
7. *Add the potatoes, cut side down, and garlic to the skillet; season with salt and pepper and cook for 5 minutes or until golden brown.*
8. *Return the chicken to skillet then snip the rosemary and oregano over the chicken using the **KITCHEN SHEARS**.*
9. *Add the wine and stock to the skillet; stir well then cover and cook for 10 minutes or until chicken is cooked through and potatoes are tender.*
10. *Add the peas to the skillet.*
11. *Use the **CITRUS ZESTER** to zest the lemon over the chicken.*
12. *Use the **BIRDS BEAK GARNISHING KNIFE** to cut the lemon in half then squeeze the juice over the chicken.*
13. *Stir, remove from heat and garnish as desired before serving.*

ONE SKILLET
CHICKEN STEW

Makes 4 servings

Ingredients:

4 boneless, skinless chicken breasts
1 large yellow onion
2 large potatoes
2 carrots
2 celery stalks
Kosher salt and fresh pepper to taste
1/2 cup all purpose flour
2 tablespoons canola oil
4 cups chicken stock
1 bay leaf

Method:

1. Use the **CRINKLE CUTTER** to cut chicken into 1-inch pieces.
2. Use the **BIRDS BEAK GARNISHING KNIFE** to peel the onion then chop it using the **CRINKLE CUTTER**.
3. Use the **Y-PEELER** to peel the potatoes and carrots.
4. Use the **BIRDS BEAK GARNISHING KNIFE** to cut the potatoes into 1/2-inch pieces, the carrots into 1/4-inch coins and the celery into 1/4-inch pieces.
5. Season chicken with salt and pepper then dredge the chicken in flour.
6. Preheat the oil in a large skillet over medium-high heat.
7. When oil is hot, add the chicken to the skillet; sear on all sides for 3-4 minutes or until browned.
8. Add the onions, potatoes, carrots, celery, stock and bay leaf; cover with lid.
9. Reduce heat to low and cook for 10-15 minutes or until chicken is tender and cooked through.
10. Garnish and adjust seasoning as desired before serving.

GREG'S EASY CHICKEN SOUP

Makes 2-4 servings

Ingredients:

1 tablespoon canola oil
2 carrots
1 small yellow onion
1 celery stalk
1 bay leaf
1 pound rotisserie chicken meat, cooked
1 quart chicken stock
Kosher salt and fresh pepper to taste

Method:

1. *Preheat the oil in a small stockpot over medium heat.*
2. *Use the **Y-PEELER** to peel the carrots then slice using the **BIRDS BEAK GARNISHING KNIFE**.*
3. *Use the **BIRDS BEAK GARNISHING KNIFE** to peel the onion then chop it using the **STAINLESS STEEL CHOPPER**.*
4. *Use the **STAINLESS STEEL CHOPPER** to chop the celery and chicken.*
5. *Use the **STAINLESS STEEL CHOPPER** to scoop and transfer the carrots, onions and celery to the stockpot; add the bay leaf then cook for 5 minutes or until tender.*
6. *Add the chicken to the stockpot; stir and cook for an additional 3 minutes.*
7. *Add the stock then season with salt and pepper; cook for an additional 15 minutes.*
8. *Adjust seasoning, garnish as desired and serve.*

BBQ CHICKEN
QUESADILLAS

Makes 2 servings

Ingredients:

2 flour tortillas
1/4 cup bottled BBQ sauce
1/2 cup leftover rotisserie chicken
4-ounce block Monterrey Jack cheese
1 small red onion
1/2 jalapeño pepper
2 tablespoons cilantro (optional)

Method:

1. *Preheat a large skillet over medium heat.*
2. *Place one tortilla on a cutting board and spread evenly with BBQ sauce.*
3. *Use the **STAINLESS STEEL CHOPPER** to chop the chicken.*
4. *Use the **FINE GRATER** to grate the cheese.*
5. *Use the **BIRDS BEAK GARNISHING KNIFE** to peel the onion then thinly slice it using the **CRINKLE CUTTER**.*
6. *Use the **BIRDS BEAK GARNISHING KNIFE** to seed and slice the jalapeño pepper.*
7. *Top tortilla evenly with the chicken, red onions, cheese and jalapeño peppers.*
8. *Cover with second tortilla.*
9. *Apply nonstick spray to the skillet.*
10. *Place the quesadilla in the skillet; cook for 2 minutes on each side or until cheese is melted.*
11. *When cooking is complete, transfer quesadilla to a cutting board then cut into wedges.*
12. *Use the **KITCHEN SHEARS** to snip the cilantro for garnishing if desired before serving.*

CHICKEN
STROGANOFF

Makes 4 servings

Ingredients:

1 small onion
4 ounces button mushrooms
1 1/4 pounds boneless, skinless chicken breasts
2 tablespoons unsalted butter
2 tablespoons all purpose flour
1 teaspoon paprika
Kosher salt and fresh pepper to taste
1 cup chicken stock
1 tablespoon Worcestershire sauce
1/2 cup sour cream
12 ounces egg noodles, cooked
Fresh parsley for garnish

Method:

1. *Use the **BIRDS BEAK GARNISHING KNIFE** to peel the onion then chop it using the **CRINKLE CUTTER**.*
2. *Use the **CRINKLE CUTTER** to slice the mushrooms 1/4-inch thick.*
3. *Use the **CRINKLE CUTTER** to cut the chicken into 1-inch chunks; set aside.*
4. *Melt the butter in a large sauté pan over medium-high heat.*
5. *Use the **STAINLESS STEEL CHOPPER** to scoop and transfer the onions to the pan; cook for 2 minutes or until softened.*
6. *Add the mushrooms and cook for 2 minutes or until mushrooms are browned.*
7. *Add the chicken, flour, paprika, salt and pepper; cook and stir for 3 minutes or until chicken is browned.*
8. *Add the stock and Worcestershire sauce; bring to a simmer for 5 minutes.*
9. *Add the sour cream; stir then adjust seasoning if desired.*
10. *Cook for an additional 2-3 minutes or until chicken is done.*
11. *Serve over egg noodles.*
12. *Use the **KITCHEN SHEARS** to snip fresh parsley for garnishing before serving.*

CHICKEN & NOODLES

Makes 4 servings

For the Chicken:

4 boneless, skinless chicken breasts
2 large carrots
1 large yellow onion
2 celery stalks
3 fresh sage leaves
2 tablespoons unsalted butter
4 cups good quality chicken stock
2 bay leaves
Kosher salt and fresh pepper to taste
1 cup frozen peas, thawed
Mashed potatoes for serving (optional)

For the Noodles:

A handful of flat leaf parsley
1 bunch green onions
2/3 cup all purpose flour
1 large egg
1/2 teaspoon kosher salt
2 tablespoons unsalted butter, melted

Method:

1. Use the **CRINKLE CUTTER** to cut the chicken breasts into squares then transfer chicken to a large stockpot.
2. Use the **Y-PEELER** to peel the carrots then chop them using the **CRINKLE CUTTER**.
3. Use the **STAINLESS STEEL CHOPPER** to scoop and transfer carrots onto the chicken.
4. Use the **BIRDS BEAK GARNISHING KNIFE** to peel the onion then chop it using the **CRINKLE CUTTER**.
5. Use the **STAINLESS STEEL CHOPPER** to scoop and transfer the onions to the stockpot.
6. Use the **CRINKLE CUTTER** to chop the celery then use the **STAINLESS STEEL CHOPPER** to scoop and transfer the celery into the stockpot.
7. Use the **KITCHEN SHEARS** to snip the sage leaves into the stockpot.
8. Add the butter, stock and bay leaves to the stockpot; season well with salt and pepper.
9. Set stove to medium-high heat and simmer for 20 minutes, stirring occasionally.
10. While simmering, use the **KITCHEN SHEARS** to snip the parsley and green onions into a mixing bowl then add remaining noodle ingredients to the bowl; stir until a dough ball forms.
11. Roll out the dough on a lightly floured surface until 1/2-inch thick then use the **PASTRY WHEEL** to cut the dough into wide noodles; use the **STAINLESS STEEL CHOPPER** to scoop and transfer the noodles to the bubbling chicken mixture then cover with lid.
12. Cook noodles for 10 minutes; add the peas, stir well then adjust seasoning if desired.
13. Garnish as desired and serve hot with mashed potatoes if desired.

CHICKEN WITH PEANUT SAUCE

Makes 4 servings

For the Peanut Sauce:

2 garlic cloves
1 lime, juice and zest
1 Thai bird chili pepper, or to taste
1/2 cup crunchy peanut butter
1 tablespoon granulated sugar
1 teaspoon fish sauce
1/4 cup coconut milk

For the Chicken:

2 tablespoons canola oil
4 boneless, skinless chicken breasts
Kosher salt and fresh pepper to taste
Cooked rice for serving
Parsley for garnish

Method:

1. Use the **STAINLESS STEEL CHOPPER** to smash and chop the garlic.
2. Use the **CITRUS ZESTER** to zest the lime.
3. Place the garlic, lime zest, lime juice and remaining peanut sauce ingredients in a small saucepan; cook over medium heat until simmering then reduce heat to low and cook for an additional 5 minutes.
4. Preheat the oil a large sauté pan over medium-high heat.
5. Season the chicken with salt and pepper then transfer to the sauté pan; cook for 5 - 6 minutes on each side or until internal temperature reaches 165°F on a meat thermometer.
6. Place chicken on top of rice.
7. Spoon the peanut sauce over the chicken.
8. Use the **KITCHEN SHEARS** to snip the parsley for garnish before serving.

EASY PORK ROAST
WITH APPLES

Makes 4-6 servings

Ingredients:

2 Granny Smith apples
1 medium yellow onion
5 garlic cloves
3 tablespoons unsalted butter
3 pounds pork shoulder or butt
Kosher salt and fresh pepper to taste
1 tablespoon chicken bouillon powder such as Maggi
8 fresh sage leaves
1/3 cup light brown sugar, packed
2 cups apple juice
1 tablespoon apple cider vinegar
Green onions for garnish

Method:

1. *Preheat oven to 325°F.*
2. *Use the **APPLE CORER** to core the apples then use the **Y-PEELER** to peel them.*
3. *Use the **BIRDS BEAK GARNISHING KNIFE** to thickly slice the apples.*
4. *Use the **BIRDS BEAK GARNISHING KNIFE** to peel the onion then chop thickly using the **STAINLESS STEEL CHOPPER**.*
5. *Use the **FINE GRATER** to grate the garlic.*
6. *Melt the butter in a roasting pan or Dutch oven over medium-high heat on the stove.*
7. *Season pork with salt and pepper then place in the pan; sear on both sides until well browned.*
8. *Add remaining ingredients, except green onions, to the pan; cover with aluminum foil.*
9. *Place the pan in the oven and cook for 3-3 1/2 hours or until pork is fork tender.*
10. *When cooking is complete, remove from oven and adjust seasoning if desired.*
11. *Pull pork apart using tongs then use the **KITCHEN SHEARS** to snip the green onions for garnishing before serving.*

TIP

If you wish to thicken the juices into gravy before serving, remove the pork to a platter, place the pan on the stove over medium-high heat then stir in 2 tablespoons of cornstarch that has been dissolved in 3 tablespoons of cold water once boiling. Stir until it boils again and has thickened.

SMOTHERED PORK
CHOPS

Makes 4 servings

Ingredients:

1 bacon slice
2 large yellow onions
2 garlic cloves
4 bone-in pork chops, 6 ounces each
Kosher salt and fresh pepper to taste
1 tablespoon unsalted butter
1/4 teaspoon dried sage
4 tablespoons all purpose flour
1/3 cup whole milk
2 cups chicken stock
1 green onion
Cheesy mashed potatoes (see recipe on page 67)

Method:

1. *Use the **KITCHEN SHEARS** to cut the bacon into pieces; set aside.*
2. *Use the **BIRDS BEAK GARNISHING KNIFE** to peel the onions then thinly slice them using the **STAINLESS STEEL CHOPPER**.*
3. *Use the **STAINLESS STEEL CHOPPER** to smash and chop the garlic.*
4. *Pat pork chops thoroughly dry using paper towels then season with salt and pepper.*
5. *Melt the butter in a large sauté pan over medium-high heat.*
6. *When butter sizzles, add the pork chops and bacon to the pan.*
7. *Sear pork on both sides until brown then remove the pork and bacon to a plate.*
8. *Add the onions and garlic to the pan and sauté until softened, stirring well.*
9. *Add the sage and flour and stir for 1-2 minutes.*
10. *Add the milk and stock to the pan, stir well and bring to a simmer.*
11. *Return the pork chops and any accumulated juices to the pan; cover with lid.*
12. *Reduce heat to low and simmer for 1 hour or until chops are tender.*
13. *Adjust seasoning if desired then use the **KITCHEN SHEARS** to snip green onion for garnish.*
14. *Serve hot over mashed potatoes.*

ROOT BEER
PULLED PORK

Makes 4-6 servings

Ingredients:

2 1/2 pounds pork shoulder or butt
1 large yellow onion
1 garlic clove
1 large carrot
1/4 cup granulated sugar
1 1/2 cups root beer
1 teaspoon root beer extract (optional)

1 cup bottled BBQ sauce
Kosher salt and fresh pepper to taste
Handful of fresh parsley
1 bunch green onions
Soft buns
Coleslaw

Method:

1. *Preheat oven to 325°F.*
2. *Place the pork into a Dutch oven.*
3. *Use the **BIRDS BEAK GARNISHING KNIFE** to peel the onion then chop it using the **CRINKLE CUTTER**.*
4. *Use the **STAINLESS STEEL CHOPPER** to smash and chop the garlic.*
5. *Use the **Y-PEELER** to peel the carrot then chop it using the **CRINKLE CUTTER**.*
6. *Place the onions, garlic and carrots in the Dutch oven.*
7. *Add the sugar, root beer, extract, BBQ sauce, salt and pepper to the Dutch oven; stir.*
8. *Cover with lid then place in the oven for 3 hours or until meat is fall-apart tender.*
9. *Remove from oven then use tongs to pull meat into shreds; stir shredded meat into the sauce.*
10. *Use the **KITCHEN SHEARS** to snip the parsley and green onions over the meat; stir.*
11. *Serve on buns with coleslaw on top.*

PORK TENDERLOIN WITH
LEMON & SAGE

Makes 4 servings

For the Marinade:

2 lemons
2 garlic cloves
4 sage leaves
1 medium tomato
1/2 cup olive oil

For the Pork:

2 pounds pork tenderloin, cut 1-inch thick
Kosher salt and fresh pepper to taste
1 tablespoon olive oil
4 large basil leaves
Cooked rice for serving

Method:

1. Use the **CITRUS ZESTER** to zest the lemon into a bowl.
2. Squeeze the juice from both lemons into the bowl.
3. Use the **STAINLESS STEEL CHOPPER** to smash and chop the garlic; add to bowl.
4. Use the **CRINKLE CUTTER** to chop the sage leaves; add to bowl.
5. Use the serrated end of the **DUAL MELON BALLER** to core the tomato then chop it using the **CRINKLE CUTTER**.
6. Add the sage, tomatoes and oil to the bowl; stir to combine.
7. Season pork with salt and pepper then toss in 4 tablespoons of marinade to coat.
8. Preheat the oil in a large sauté pan over medium-high heat.
9. When oil is hot, add the pork and cook until browned on both sides and internal temperature reaches 145°F on a meat thermometer.
10. When grilling is complete, drizzle with additional marinade then plate the pork over rice.
11. Use the **KITCHEN SHEARS** to snip the basil leaves over the dish then garnish as desired before serving.

44

SWEET & SOUR
PORK

Makes 4-6 servings

Ingredients:

1 medium yellow onion
2 carrots
3 garlic cloves
2 tablespoons fresh ginger
6 tablespoons rice wine vinegar
4 tablespoons ketchup
6 tablespoons sugar
6 tablespoons soy sauce
1 tablespoon cornstarch
1 can (15.25 ounces) tropical mixed fruit (pineapple, papaya, peaches), juice reserved
2 tablespoons canola oil
1 pound pork loin chop
Cooked rice for serving (optional)

Method:

1. *Use the **BIRDS BEAK GARNISHING KNIFE** to peel the onion then chop it using the **CRINKLE CUTTER**.*
2. *Use the **Y-PEELER** to peel the carrots then cut 1/4-inch thick on the bias using the **CRINKLE CUTTER**.*
3. *Use the **STAINLESS STEEL CHOPPER** to smash and chop the garlic.*
4. *Use the **BIRDS BEAK GARNISHING KNIFE** to peel the ginger then chop it using the **CRINKLE CUTTER**.*
5. *In a bowl, whisk together the vinegar, ketchup, sugar, soy sauce, cornstarch and 1/3 cup of juice from the tropical mixed fruit can; set aside.*
6. *Preheat the oil in a large sauté pan over high heat.*
7. *Pat the pork dry using paper towels then cut into 1/4-inch strips using the **CRINKLE CUTTER**.*
8. *When oil is hot, place half of the pork into the pan and cook for 1-2 minutes on each side or until well browned; transfer to a bowl then repeat with remaining pork.*
9. *Add the onions, carrots, garlic and ginger to the pan; cook for 4 minutes.*
10. *Add the fruit juice mixture, tropical mixed fruit and pork to the pan; stir to combine then cook for 2-3 minutes or until thickened.*
11. *When cooking is complete, remove from pan and serve over rice if desired.*

SAUSAGE & SAUERKRAUT

Makes 2-4 servings

Ingredients:

1 carrot
4 small red skinned potatoes, scrubbed
1 pound kielbasa sausage
1 bag (1 pound) fresh sauerkraut, drained
1 cup beer, chicken stock or water
Fresh parsley for garnish

Method:

1. *Use the **Y-PEELER** to peel the carrot.*
2. *Use the **CRINKLE CUTTER** to cut the carrot into 1-inch coins then quarter the potatoes using the **BIRDS BEAK GARNISHING KNIFE**.*
3. *Use the **BIRDS BEAK GARNISHING KNIFE** to cut the sausage into 4 pieces.*
4. *Place all ingredients into a stockpot; cover with lid and cook over medium heat for 20 minutes or until potatoes and carrots are tender.*
5. *Use the **KITCHEN SHEARS** to snip parsley for garnishing before serving.*

SAUSAGE & CHEESE
CASSEROLE

Makes 4-6 servings

Ingredients:

1 pound breakfast sausage
1 small yellow onion
1/2 loaf Italian bread
2 Russet potatoes
4 sprigs fresh parsley
1 green bell pepper
1 tablespoon unsalted butter, softened
6 large eggs, beaten
Kosher salt and fresh pepper to taste
3 cups half & half
1 teaspoon apple cider vinegar
4 ounce block sharp Cheddar cheese
1 ounce block Parmesan cheese

Method:

1. Use the **BIRDS BEAK GARNISHING KNIFE** to slice the sausage.
2. Preheat a large skillet over medium heat; add the sausage to brown.
3. Use the **BIRDS BEAK GARNISHING KNIFE** to peel the onion then chop it using the **CRINKLE CUTTER;** add onions to the skillet.
4. Use the **CRINKLE CUTTER** to cube the bread then add to skillet.
5. Use the **CRINKLE CUTTER** to cube the potatoes and chop the parsley; add to the skillet (reserve some parsley for garnish).
6. Use the **CRINKLE CUTTER** to julienne the bell pepper then add to the skillet.
7. Add the butter, eggs, salt, pepper, half & half and vinegar; stir gently, pushing the eggs from the edge to the center, allowing the liquid part of the egg to flow under the cooked part.
8. Reduce heat to low and continue to cook until mixture is mostly set; remove from heat.
9. Use the **FINE GRATER** to grate both cheeses.
10. Add cheeses to the skillet, cover and cook for 5 minutes or until melted.
11. Garnish with additional parsley before serving.

WOLF'S REISFLEISCH

Makes 6 servings

Ingredients:

1 large yellow onion
1 garlic clove
1 large carrot
1 celery stalk
1 bell pepper, any color
1 pound smoked sausage
4 tablespoons unsalted butter
2 cups uncooked long grain rice
4 cups chicken stock
2 teaspoons fresh lemon juice
1 tablespoon paprika
Kosher salt and fresh pepper to taste
Chili flakes to taste
Fresh parsley

Method:

1. Use the **BIRDS BEAK GARNISHING KNIFE** to peel the onion then chop it using the **STAINLESS STEEL CHOPPER**.

2. Use the **STAINLESS STEEL CHOPPER** to smash and chop the garlic.

3. Use the **Y-PEELER** to peel the carrot then chop the carrot, celery and bell peppers using the **CRINKLE CUTTER**.

4. Use the **BIRDS BEAK GARNISHING KNIFE** to slice the sausage into chunks; set aside.

5. Melt the butter in a large stockpot over medium heat.

6. When butter is melted, add the rice and stir to coat for 3 minutes.

7. Add the vegetables and stir for 2-3 minutes or until vegetables are tender.

8. Add the sausage and remaining ingredients, except parsley; stir well and cook for 15 minutes.

9. Reduce heat to low, cover and cook for an additional 10 minutes.

10. Use the **KITCHEN SHEARS** to snip the parsley for garnish.

11. Fluff rice and serve hot.

PORK STEW

Makes 4-6 servings

Ingredients:

2 small sweet potatoes
1 large yellow onion
2 whole carrots
1 celery stalk
4 garlic cloves
4 pounds pork shoulder
1 tablespoon canola oil
Kosher salt and fresh pepper to taste
4 cups good quality chicken stock
2 teaspoons minute tapioca
1 bay leaf
2 tablespoons ketchup
12 ounces beer or chicken stock
Parsley for garnish

Method:

1. Use the **Y-PEELER** to peel the potatoes then cut into 3/4-inch cubes using the **BIRDS BEAK GARNISHING KNIFE**.
2. Use the **BIRDS BEAK GARNISHING KNIFE** to peel the onion then slice it using the **CRINKLE CUTTER.**
3. Use the **Y-PEELER** to peel the carrots then cut carrots and celery into 1-inch pieces using the **CRINKLE CUTTER**.
4. Use the **STAINLESS STEEL CHOPPER** to smash and chop the garlic.
5. Use the **CRINKLE CUTTER** to cut the pork into 1-inch cubes.
6. Preheat the oil in a Dutch oven over medium-high heat.
7. When oil is hot, add the pork and sear on all sides until browned; season with salt and pepper.
8. Add remaining ingredients, except parsley, to the Dutch oven; stir well then turn heat to low.
9. Simmer for 2 hours or until pork is tender.
10. Adjust seasoning if desired then snip parsley over the stew using the **KITCHEN SHEARS** before serving.

HONEY GLAZED
PORK CHOPS

Makes 4 servings

Ingredients:

1 orange
3 sprigs fresh thyme
4 fresh sage leaves
1 tablespoon olive oil
1 teaspoon Worcestershire sauce
Kosher salt and fresh pepper to taste
4 pork chops, cut 3/4-inch thick
2 tablespoons honey

Method:

1. *Preheat oven to 375°F.*
2. *Use the **FINE GRATER** to zest the orange into a bowl.*
3. *Squeeze the juice from the orange into the bowl.*
4. *Use the **CRINKLE CUTTER** to chop the thyme and sage; add to the bowl.*
5. *Add the olive oil and Worcestershire sauce to the bowl; stir and set aside.*
6. *Pierce the pork chops in several places using a fork then season with salt and pepper.*
7. *Dip the pork chops in the orange mixture then coat both sides.*
8. *Place the pork chops on a rack then set the rack on a rimmed cookie sheet.*
9. *Place in the oven for 15 minutes, turn chops then cook for an additional 10 minutes.*
10. *While pork chops are in the oven, whisk the honey into the remaining orange mixture.*
11. *Brush the chops with orange mixture then cook for an additional 10 minutes or until internal temperature reaches 145°F on a meat thermometer.*
12. *When cooking is complete garnish as desired and serve.*

ONE SKILLET TUNA
CASSEROLE

Makes 4-6 servings

Ingredients:

1 large yellow onion
2 celery stalks
1 tablespoon unsalted butter
2 cans (7 ounces each) tuna, drained
2 cups dry long grain white rice
1 cup chicken stock
3/4 cup whole milk
2 ounces cream cheese, softened
Kosher salt and fresh pepper to taste
10 ounces frozen peas, thawed
4-ounce block of Cheddar cheese
1 bunch green onions

Method:

1. *Preheat a large skillet over medium-high heat.*
2. *Use the **BIRDS BEAK GARNISHING KNIFE** to peel the onion then chop the onion and celery using the **CRINKLE CUTTER**.*
3. *Add the butter to the skillet then use the **STAINLESS STEEL CHOPPER** to scoop and transfer the onions and celery to the skillet; cook for 5 minutes.*
4. *Add the tuna, rice, stock, milk and cream cheese to the skillet; bring to a boil.*
5. *Cover and simmer for 15 minutes, stirring occasionally until rice is just tender.*
6. *Remove from heat, season to taste with salt and pepper then add the peas.*
7. *Use the **FINE GRATER** to grate the cheese over the skillet; let stand for 5 minutes to melt the cheese or place under the broiler for 2-3 minutes or until lightly browned.*
8. *Use the **KITCHEN SHEARS** to snip green onions for garnishing before serving.*

SALMON & MUSHROOM
BROWN RICE

Makes 2 servings

For the Steamed Salmon:

1 green onion
2 teaspoons fresh ginger
1 garlic clove
2 salmon fillets, 4 ounces each
1 tablespoon soy sauce

For the Rice:

2/3 cup brown rice
1 1/4 cups stock or water
1 bay leaf
2 teaspoons olive oil
1/2 cup dried shiitake mushrooms (rehydrated
in 1 cup hot water, squeezed to remove excess water)
2 teaspoons soy sauce
1 garlic clove, smashed
1/2 teaspoon chili flakes
Kosher salt and fresh pepper to taste
1 green onion

Method:

1. *Use the **KITCHEN SHEARS** to snip the green onion for the salmon.*
2. *Use the **BIRDS BEAK GARNISHING KNIFE** to remove the skin from the ginger then chop it.*
3. *Use the **STAINLESS STEEL CHOPPER** to smash and chop the garlic.*
4. *Rub salmon with soy sauce.*
5. *Top salmon evenly with green onions, garlic and ginger; let marinate for 10 minutes.*
6. *Place all rice ingredients, except green onion, into a saucepan.*
7. *Bring to a boil over medium heat then simmer for 10 minutes before reducing heat to low.*
8. *Use the **KITCHEN SHEARS** to snip the green onion for the rice.*
9. *Top rice with salmon and green onions; cover and cook for an additional 7 - 10 minutes or until salmon is cooked to desired doneness.*
10. *Garnish as desired and serve salmon over rice.*

SHRIMP & GRITS

Makes 3-4 servings

For the Grits:

4 cups water
1 teaspoon kosher salt
1 cup stone ground grits
4 tablespoons butter, divided

For the Shrimp:

1 tablespoon olive oil
1 1/2 pounds large shrimp, peeled and deveined
Kosher salt and fresh pepper to taste
1 garlic clove
1 corn on the cob
1 bunch green onions for garnish
1/2 teaspoon chili flakes

Method:

1. *Pour water and salt into a stockpot; bring water to a boil over high heat.*
2. *Whisk in the grits, reduce heat to low then cover and cook for 5 minutes or until grits are tender; remove from heat, stir in 2 tablespoons butter and set aside.*
3. *Preheat the olive oil and remaining butter in a large sauté pan over medium-high heat.*
4. *Pat shrimp dry, season with salt and pepper then add to the pan; toss shrimp for 3 minutes or until heated through then remove from heat (do not over cook).*
5. *Use the **STAINLESS STEEL CHOPPER** to smash and chop the garlic.*
6. *Use the **BIRDS BEAK GARNISHING KNIFE** to cut the corn from the cob.*
7. *Use the **KITCHEN SHEARS** to snip the green onions.*
8. *Add the corn, garlic, chili flakes and green onions to the pan; stir and cook for 1 minute or until vegetables are soft and fragrant.*
9. *Serve grits in bowls, topped with shrimp and garlic mixture.*

CRABBY APPETIZER
ROLLS

Makes 12 rolls

Ingredients:

8 ounces lump fresh crab meat (use imitation if desired)
1 bunch fresh chives
1 can (8 ounces) whole water chestnuts
1/4 red bell pepper
3 tablespoons mayonnaise
2 English cucumbers
1 teaspoon black sesame seeds

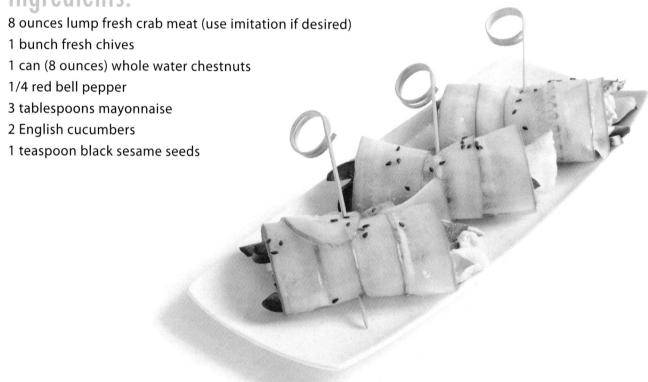

Method:

1. *Place the crab meat in a bowl then remove all bits of shell.*
2. *Use the **KITCHEN SHEARS** to finely snip the chives over the crab meat.*
3. *Use the **CRINKLE CUTTER** to finely chop the water chestnuts then add to the bowl.*
4. *Use the **BIRDS BEAK GARNISHING KNIFE** to slice the bell pepper into very thin strips then add to the bowl.*
5. *Stir the mayonnaise into the crab mixture.*
6. *Use the **Y-PEELER** to peel lengthwise strips from the cucumbers.*
7. *Place a small spoonful of crab mixture on one end of a cucumber strip.*
8. *Roll it up then secure end with a small skewer; repeat to make additional rolls.*
9. *Sprinkle with sesame seeds before serving.*

CREAM CHEESE STUFFED
GRAPE APPETIZERS

Makes 6-10 servings

Ingredients:

24 large red or green grapes
1/4 cup pistachio nuts, toasted
8 ounces cream cheese
Kosher salt and fresh pepper to taste
Chives (optional)
2 tablespoons honey

Method:

1. Use the **BIRDS BEAK GARNISHING KNIFE** to trim the bottom off each grape so they sit flat.
2. Use the **APPLE CORER** to remove the top from each grape.
3. Use the **STAINLESS STEEL CHOPPER** to finely chop the pistachio nuts.
4. Dip the cut side of each grape in the nuts then place the grapes on a serving tray.
5. In a bowl, combine the cream cheese, salt and pepper.
6. Use the **KITCHEN SHEARS** to snip chives over the cream cheese if desired; stir to combine.
7. Use the **DUAL MELON BALLER** to divide the mixture into 24 small balls.
8. Roll each ball over a piece of cheesecloth for a decorative edge if desired.
9. Fill each grape with a cream cheese ball.
10. Use the **KITCHEN SHEARS** to snip additional chives over the grapes if desired.
11. Season grapes with salt and pepper.
12. Drizzle with honey before serving.

SKINNY CHIPS & SALSA

Makes 6 servings

Ingredients:

6 large ripe tomatoes
1 garlic clove
1 large white onion
A handful of fresh cilantro
2 limes, zest and juice
1-2 serrano chili peppers
Kosher salt to taste
2 English cucumbers
1 jicama bulb (optional)

Method:

1. Use the serrated end of the **DUAL MELON BALLER** to remove the core from the tomatoes.
2. Use the **BIRDS BEAK GARNISHING KNIFE** to dice the tomatoes then transfer to a bowl.
3. Use the **STAINLESS STEEL CHOPPER** to smash and chop the garlic; transfer to the bowl.
4. Use the **BIRDS BEAK GARNISHING KNIFE** to peel the onion then chop using the **CRINKLE CUTTER**; transfer to the bowl.
5. Use the **KITCHEN SHEARS** to snip the cilantro over the tomato mixture.
6. Use the **CITRUS ZESTER** to zest the limes into the bowl.
7. Use the **BIRDS BEAK GARNISHING KNIFE** to cut limes in half then squeeze juice into the bowl.
8. Use the **BIRDS BEAK GARNISHING KNIFE** to seed and slice the chili peppers; add to the bowl.
9. Season with salt if desired.
10. Use the **CRINKLE CUTTER** to slice the cucumber into "chips".
11. Use the **Y-PEELER** to peel the jicama, cut into 4 chunks using the **BIRDS BEAK GARNISHING KNIFE** then cut into "chips" using the **CRINKLE CUTTER**.
12. Serve salsa with cucumber and jicama chips.

BUTTERNUT SQUASH SOUP

Makes 6 servings

Ingredients:

2 pounds butternut squash
1 large yellow onion
2 tablespoons unsalted butter
1 tablespoon olive oil
3 cups chicken stock
2 teaspoons apple cider vinegar
2 teaspoons kosher salt
1/2 teaspoon fresh pepper
1 cinnamon stick
1 cup half & half or milk
Chives for garnish
1 tablespoon honey

Method:

1. *Use the **Y-PEELER** to peel the squash then use the **CRINKLE CUTTER** to cut into chunks.*
2. *Use the **BIRDS BEAK GARNISHING KNIFE** to peel the onion then chop it using the **CRINKLE CUTTER**.*
3. *In an 8 quart stockpot over medium heat, melt the butter and heat the oil.*
4. *Add the onions and cook for 5 minutes or until translucent.*
5. *Add butternut squash, chicken stock, vinegar, salt and pepper.*
6. *Use the **FINE GRATER** to grate the cinnamon into the soup; cover with lid.*
7. *Reduce heat to medium-low and let simmer for 30 minutes or until butternut squash is fork tender.*
8. *Transfer 1/3 of the squash mixture to a blender; cover with lid.*
9. *Puree on low speed to avoid splashing then increase speed to high and puree until smooth.*
10. *Pour into a serving tureen and repeat with remaining squash mixture.*
11. *Add the half & half or milk; stir until combined.*
12. *Ladle into bowls.*
13. *Use the **KITCHEN SHEARS** to snip the chives for garnish.*
14. *Drizzle soup with honey before serving.*

ZUCCHINI LATKES

Makes 4 servings

Ingredients:

2 cups zucchini, raw
1/2 cup yellow onion
1/4 cup celery leaves
3 green onions
3 large eggs
1/3 cup all purpose flour
Kosher salt and fresh pepper to taste
3 tablespoons canola oil
Sour cream for serving

Method:

1. *Use the **FINE GRATER** to grate the zucchini then pat dry using paper towels.*
2. *Use the **BIRDS BEAK GARNISHING KNIFE** to peel the onion then grate it using the **FINE GRATER**.*
3. *Use the **KITCHEN SHEARS** to snip the celery leaves and green onions.*
4. *Preheat a large skillet over medium heat.*
5. *Wrap grated onions in a double layer of paper towels and squeeze out excess water.*
6. *In a mixing bowl stir together the zucchini, onions, celery and green onions.*
7. *Stir in the eggs, flour and salt and pepper.*
8. *Brush skillet with some of the oil.*
9. *Drop zucchini mixture into the skillet using 1 tablespoon per latke.*
10. *Pat down tops to flatten a bit and cook for 2-3 minutes on each side or until well browned.*
11. *Remove and repeat with any remaining mixture.*
12. *Serve hot with sour cream.*

TIP

It is important to remove any excess moisture from the zucchini and onions, otherwise the patties fall apart and will not get crispy.

MAC & CHEESE

Makes 6 servings

Ingredients:

5-ounce block mozzarella cheese

6-ounce block extra sharp Cheddar cheese

2-ounce block Monterey Jack cheese

2-ounce wedge of Parmesan cheese

1 cup Cheddar cheese for topping

7 cups elbow or other small pasta, cooked

1/2 cup chicken stock

1/2 cup half & half

1 tablespoon unsalted butter

1 teaspoon dry mustard

A pinch of cayenne pepper

1 teaspoon kosher salt or to taste

1 tablespoon ketchup

Chives for garnish

Method:

1. *Use the **FINE GRATER** to grate all the cheeses; set aside 1 cup Cheddar cheese for topping.*

2. *Preheat oven to 350°F.*

3. *In a bowl, combine all ingredients, except chives and reserved Cheddar cheese; gently stir to combine.*

4. *Divide the mixture between small casserole dishes or cocottes then top with reserved cheese.*

5. *Bake for 30-40 minutes or until bubbly and top is golden brown.*

6. *Use the **KITCHEN SHEARS** to snip chives for garnishing before serving.*

QUINOA
PILAF

Makes 6 servings

For the Quinoa:

1 small yellow onion
1/2 cup dried apricots
2 cups quinoa
1 3/4 cups water
1 tablespoon chicken bouillon powder
1 tablespoon soy sauce
2 tablespoons olive oil
1/2 teaspoon dried thyme
1 cup sliced almonds, toasted
1 cup raisins
1/2 teaspoon chili flakes or to taste

For Serving:

1 bunch green onions
2 tablespoons parsley
1 lemon, zest and juice
1 cup red grapes
Kosher salt and fresh pepper to taste

Method:

1. *Use the **BIRDS BEAK GARNISHING KNIFE** to peel the onion then chop it using the **STAINLESS STEEL CHOPPER**.*
2. *Use the **STAINLESS STEEL CHOPPER** to chop the apricots.*
3. *Preheat a stockpot over medium-high heat.*
4. *Using a fine strainer, rinse the quinoa for 1 minute to remove the bitter natural coating.*
5. *Place all quinoa ingredients into the stockpot; cover with lid and cook for 15 minutes.*
6. *While quinoa is cooking, use the **KITCHEN SHEARS** to snip the green onions and parsley.*
7. *Use the **CITRUS ZESTER** to zest the lemon.*
8. *Cut lemon in half using the **BIRDS BEAK GARNISHING KNIFE** then squeeze the juice into a small bowl.*
9. *Use the **BIRDS BEAK GARNISHING KNIFE** to cut the grapes in half.*
10. *When cooking is complete, add all ingredients for serving to the stockpot; stir.*
11. *Taste and adjust seasoning if desired.*
12. *Serve hot or cold.*

RECIPES

EGGPLANT
STACK

Makes 2 servings

Ingredients:

1 small eggplant
2-ounce block Parmesan cheese
2 balls fresh mozzarella cheese
6 fresh basil leaves
1 large egg, beaten
1/4 cup tomato sauce

Method:

1. Use the **CHANNEL KNIFE** to score the sides of the eggplant before slicing.
2. Use the **CRINKLE CUTTER** to slice the eggplant into 1/2-inch thick rounds.
3. Use the **FINE GRATER** to grate the Parmesan cheese.
4. Use the **STAINLESS STEEL CHOPPER** to cut mozzarella into 1/2-inch thick slices.
5. Use the **KITCHEN SHEARS** to julienne the basil.
6. Preheat a grill pan over medium heat.
7. Pour the beaten egg into a bowl.
8. Place the Parmesan cheese into a separate bowl.
9. Dip the eggplant slices first into the egg then roll them in Parmesan cheese until coated.
10. Apply nonstick spray to the grill pan.
11. Place 1 eggplant slice in the grill pan; cook for 2-3 minutes on each side or until brown.
12. Repeat with remaining eggplant slices.
13. To assemble, layer the eggplant slices with mozzarella slices and basil leaves.
14. Serve over tomato sauce.

TIP

I like to substitute yellow squash or zucchini for the eggplant when they are in season.

VEGETARIAN ONE POT
PASTA DINNER

Makes 4 servings

Ingredients:

1 large yellow onion

1 small butternut squash

1 celery stalk

2-ounce block Parmesan cheese

3 tablespoons unsalted butter

4 cups dry rigatoni pasta

6 cups vegetable stock

4 fresh sage leaves, torn

Kosher salt and fresh pepper to taste

3 ounces cream cheese, softened

Chives for garnish

Method:

1. *Use the **BIRDS BEAK GARNISHING KNIFE** to peel the onion then chop it using the **STAINLESS STEEL CHOPPER**.*
2. *Use the **Y-PEELER** to peel the squash then cut into chunks using the **STAINLESS STEEL CHOPPER**.*
3. *Use the **STAINLESS STEEL CHOPPER** to chop the celery.*
4. *Use the **FINE GRATER** to grate the cheese; set aside.*
5. *Melt the butter in a large stockpot over medium heat.*
6. *When butter sizzles, add the onions; stir and cook for 10 minutes or until very brown.*
7. *Add pasta, stock, sage, salt and pepper to the stockpot; stir to combine.*
8. *Cover with lid then cook for 20 minutes or until squash is tender.*
9. *Stir in the cheeses until creamy.*
10. *Use the **KITCHEN SHEARS** to snip chives for garnishing before serving.*

VEGETARIAN MUSHROOM BURGER

Makes 4 servings

For the Burgers:

2 tablespoons olive oil

1 1/2 pounds fresh cremini, button and portobello mushrooms

4 garlic cloves

1 tablespoon unsalted butter

2 teaspoons kosher salt

1/2 teaspoon freshly ground pepper

2-ounce block Parmesan cheese

1 bunch green onions

2 tablespoons cream cheese

1/2 cup breadcrumbs or panko

2 tablespoons canola oil

For Serving:

4 very soft buns

4 red onion slices

4 butter lettuce leaves

4 tablespoons mayonnaise

Method:

1. *Preheat the olive oil in a large sauté pan over medium-high heat.*
2. *Use the **STAINLESS STEEL CHOPPER** to chop the mushrooms.*
3. *Use the **STAINLESS STEEL CHOPPER** to smash and chop the garlic.*
4. *Add the mushrooms, garlic, butter, salt and pepper to the pan; stir for 10 minutes or until all the water in the mushrooms has evaporated, the mushrooms are browned and the bottom of pan is coated with brown bits.*
5. *Transfer the pan contents to a bowl and let cool.*
6. *Use the **FINE GRATER** to grate the Parmesan cheese.*
7. *Use the **KITCHEN SHEARS** to snip the green onions.*
8. *Add the cheeses, green onions and breadcrumbs to the bowl; mix and form into 4 patties; chill.*
9. *Preheat the canola oil a sauté pan over medium heat.*
10. *When oil is hot, add the patties and cook for 3-4 minutes on each side or until desired doneness.*
11. *Serve with buns with desired toppings.*

VEGGIE & PASTA SALAD

Makes 4 servings

Ingredients:

1 cup cherry tomatoes
1/2 cup fresh spinach
1 small yellow onion
1/4 cup green onions
4 cups shell or other pasta, cooked
2 tablespoons olive oil
2 tablespoons balsamic vinegar
Kosher salt and fresh pepper to taste

Method:

1. *Use the **BIRDS BEAK GARNISHING KNIFE** to cut tomatoes in half.*
2. *Use the **KITCHEN SHEARS** to julienne the spinach.*
3. *Use the **BIRDS BEAK GARNISHING KNIFE** to peel the onion then chop it using the **STAINLESS STEEL CHOPPER.***
4. *Use the **KITCHEN SHEARS** to snip the green onions.*
5. *Place all ingredients into a large bowl; toss gently to combine.*
6. *Adjust seasoning if desired.*
7. *Refrigerate for 1 hour to chill.*
8. *Garnish as desired before serving.*

HOT CHILI PEPPER
FLOWERS

For Garnishing

Ingredients:

Assorted long, thin chili peppers in various colors

Method:

1. *Wash the peppers wearing kitchen gloves if you are sensitive to chili heat.*
2. *Use the **BIRDS BEAK GARNISHING KNIFE** to make thin cuts from the chili stem to the tip.*
3. *Place the peppers in ice water for 4 hours or until peppers open up.*
4. *Use the chili pepper flowers to decorate desired foods.*

SOUTHERN POTATO
SALAD

Makes 4 servings

Ingredients:

2 pounds red skinned potatoes

1/2 small yellow onion

1 celery stalk

1 tablespoon apple cider vinegar

2 tablespoons sweet pickle relish

1/2 cup mayonnaise

2 tablespoons yellow mustard

2 large eggs, hard boiled, chopped, (optional)

Kosher salt and fresh pepper to taste

Method:

1. *Fill a stockpot with enough water to cover the potatoes; bring to a boil.*
2. *Use the **BIRDS BEAK GARNISHING KNIFE** to cut the potatoes into 1/2-inch cubes.*
3. *Place potatoes in the stockpot and cook for 20 minutes or until potatoes are tender.*
4. *While potatoes are cooking, use the **BIRDS BEAK GARNISHING KNIFE** to peel the onion then dice the onion and celery using the **STAINLESS STEEL CHOPPER**.*
5. *When potatoes are done, drain completely; set aside.*
6. *In a large bowl, combine remaining ingredients.*
7. *Add potatoes to the bowl and carefully stir to combine without mashing the potatoes.*
8. *Serve immediately or chill until serving time.*

CHEESY MASHED POTATOES

Makes 4 servings

Ingredients:

6 large Russet potatoes
5 quarts water
Kosher salt to taste
4 tablespoons unsalted butter, melted and hot
1 cup whole milk or half & half, hot
Fresh pepper to taste
Cheddar cheese
Chives

Method:

1. *Use the **Y-PEELER** to peel the potatoes then cut into cubes using the **BIRDS BEAK GARNISHING KNIFE**.*

2. *Place the potatoes and water into a large stockpot over medium-high heat; season with salt.*

3. *Cook for 20 minutes or until potatoes are fork tender.*

4. *Drain the potatoes then mash using a potato masher (pass through a ricer or food mill for a silkier consistency).*

5. *Add the butter and salt to taste then stir in enough hot milk until soft and creamy or until desired consistency (do not over mix potatoes or they will become sticky in texture).*

6. *Taste and adjust seasoning if desired.*

7. *Use the **FINE GRATER** to grate the Cheddar cheese over the potatoes then use the **KITCHEN SHEARS** to snip the chives for garnish before serving.*

SCALLOPED CORN

Makes 8 servings

Ingredients:

3 corn on the cob

3 green onions

2-ounce block Parmesan cheese

3 large eggs, beaten

20 saltine crackers, crushed

1 cup half & half

2 teaspoons sugar

2 teaspoons kosher salt

Pepper to taste

Method:

1. *Preheat oven to 350°F.*
2. *Use the **BIRDS BEAK GARNISHING KNIFE** to remove the corn kernels from the cobs.*
3. *Use the **KITCHEN SHEARS** to snip the green onions.*
4. *Use the **FINE GRATER** to grate the Parmesan cheese.*
5. *Combine all ingredients in a large bowl; mix well then pour into a greased casserole dish.*
6. *Bake for 45 minutes or until well browned.*
7. *When baking is complete, adjust seasoning and garnish as desire before serving.*

PAN ROASTED VEGGIES

Makes 4 servings

Ingredients:

8 small red potatoes

4 carrots

4 parsnips

1 large white onion

2 celery stalks

1 tablespoon olive oil

1 tablespoon unsalted butter, melted

1 tablespoon kosher salt, or to taste

1 teaspoon black pepper

Fresh herbs such as rosemary, thyme and sage (optional)

Method:

1. *Preheat oven to 400˚F.*
2. *Use the **BIRDS BEAK GARNISHING KNIFE** to cut potatoes in half.*
3. *Use the **Y-PEELER** to peel carrots and parsnips then use the **CRINKLE CUTTER** to cut both lengthwise.*
4. *Use the **BIRDS BEAK GARNISHING KNIFE** to peel the onion and then cut onion and celery into pieces using the **CRINKLE CUTTER**.*
5. *Place the vegetables and remaining ingredients into a large bowl; toss well.*
6. *Spread the bowl contents out on a roasting pan.*
7. *Place roasting pan in the oven on the bottom rack.*
8. *Bake for 1 hour or until veggies are fork tender.*
9. *Remove and serve.*

TIP
You can also use vegetables such as leeks, baby artichokes or beets.

SEVEN LAYER
SALAD

Makes 6 servings

Ingredients:

8 bacon strips
1 head iceberg lettuce
1/2 red onion
1 small cucumber
2 cups frozen peas, thawed
1 cup mayonnaise
1 tablespoon sugar
1 tablespoon yellow mustard
4-ounce block of Cheddar cheese

Method:

1. *Preheat a sauté pan over medium heat.*
2. *Use the **KITCHEN SHEARS** to snip the raw bacon into pieces.*
3. *Add bacon to the pan; cook until crisp then drain and set aside.*
4. *Use the **BIRDS BEAK GARNISHING KNIFE** to remove the core from the lettuce.*
5. *Use the **STAINLESS STEEL CHOPPER** to chop the lettuce then transfer to an 8 x 8-inch glass dish; firmly press the lettuce to the bottom of the glass dish.*
6. *Use the **CRINKLE CUTTER** to dice the onion then press into the glass dish.*
7. *Use the **Y-PEELER** to peel the cucumber then dice it using the **CRINKLE CUTTER**; press the cucumber and peas into the glass dish.*
8. *In a bowl whisk together the mayonnaise, sugar and mustard; spread mixture evenly over the ingredients in the glass dish.*
9. *Use the **FINE GRATER** to grate the Cheddar cheese over the mayonnaise mixture then top with bacon pieces.*
10. *Cover with plastic wrap and refrigerate for a minimum of 1 hour or up to 24 hours before serving.*

VEGETARIAN OMELET POCKETS

Makes 2 servings

Ingredients:

2-ounce block Parmesan cheese
1 small yellow onion
8 spinach leaves
2 tablespoons mushrooms
1/2 red bell pepper
4 large eggs
Kosher salt and fresh pepper to taste

Method:

1. *Use the **FINE GRATER** to grate the Parmesan cheese.*
2. *Use the **BIRDS BEAK GARNISHING KNIFE** to peel and slice the onion.*
3. *Use the **KITCHEN SHEARS** to julienne the spinach.*
4. *Use the **BIRDS BEAK GARNISHING KNIFE** to slice the mushrooms and bell pepper.*
5. *Preheat an omelet pan over medium heat.*
6. *In a bowl, whisk the eggs.*
7. *Apply nonstick spray to the pan then add the eggs.*
8. *Use a spatula to lift the edges as it cooks while moving the pan back and forth.*
9. *When most of the moisture is gone or when desired doneness is achieved, remove from heat.*
10. *Top omelet with onions, spinach, mushrooms, bell peppers and cheese then fold in half.*
11. *Garnish as desired and season to taste before serving.*

TIP
You can use 1 cup of egg substitute in place of the 4 large eggs.

BROWN SUGAR
BAKED APPLES

Makes 4 servings

Ingredients:

4 Pink Lady apples
4 tablespoons unsalted butter, divided
4 tablespoons dark brown sugar, packed
1/2 cup coconut flakes, toasted
1/2 cup cream of coconut
1 1/4 cups apple cider or juice

Method:

1. *Preheat oven to 350°F.*
2. *If apples do not stand up straight, trim off the bottoms using the **CRINKLE CUTTER**.*
3. *Use the **DUAL MELON BALLER** to remove the core and create a pocket (do not scoop all the way to the bottom of the apples).*
4. *Place the apples in a baking dish.*
5. *Divide the butter and brown sugar between the apples then top with coconut.*
6. *Drizzle with the cream of coconut.*
7. *Pour apple cider or juice down the side of the baking dish.*
8. *Cover the baking dish with aluminum foil then bake for 1 hour or until apples are tender.*
9. *Garnish as desired and serve warm with some of the sauce from the baking dish.*

LEMON TART WITH
MANGO RIBBONS

Makes 6 servings

Ingredients:

1 package refrigerated pie crust
1 jar store-bought lemon curd
1 lime
2 firm mangoes, unpeeled

Method:

1. *Preheat oven to 350°F.*
2. *Grease a fluted tart pan.*
3. *Unroll the pie crust dough then ease onto the tart pan without stretching.*
4. *Press the dough evenly up the sides of the pan.*
5. *Use the **PASTRY WHEEL** to trim excess dough.*
6. *Bake for 25-30 minutes or until brown around the edges; remove and let cool.*
7. *Fill cooled tart with lemon curd to just 1/4-inch below the tart's top.*
8. *Use the **CITRUS ZESTER** to zest the lime over the lemon curd.*
9. *Use the **BIRDS BEAK GARNISHING KNIFE** to cut 4 even wedges from each of the mangoes.*
10. *Use the **Y-PEELER** to slice long, thin, even "ribbons" from the mango wedges.*
11. *Roll up each "ribbon" into a coil then arrange decoratively on top of the lemon curd.*
12. *Serve tart within 2 hours or the pastry will get soggy.*

FRESH MANGO
SORBET

Makes about 1 quart

Ingredients:

4 large, very ripe mangoes
1 lime
1/2 - 2/3 cup granulated sugar (more or less depending on sweetness of mangoes)
Tiny pinch of kosher salt
Honeydew melon

Method:

1. *Use the **Y-PEELER** to peel the mangoes then cube them using the **BIRDS BEAK GARNISHING KNIFE**.*
2. *Use the **CITRUS ZESTER** to zest the lime.*
3. *Use the **BIRDS BEAK GARNISHING KNIFE** to cut lime in half then squeeze the juice into a bowl.*
4. *Use an immersion blender to puree all ingredients, except melon; strain if you prefer a smoother texture.*
5. *Chill until very cold then spin in an ice cream maker following manufacturer's instructions.*
6. *Remove and place in a covered container and freeze for 1 hour to harden.*
7. *Use the **DUAL MELON BALLER** to scoop balls from the honeydew melon for garnish.*
8. *Garnish as desired and serve.*

TIP

If you don't have an ice cream maker, pour into a 9 x 13-inch pan and freeze for 3 hours or until solid. Use a fork to break it up into chunks and a potato masher to mash it up until smooth.

GRANDMA'S
LEMON BARS

Makes 12-18 bars

For the Crust:

1 1/2 cups all purpose flour

1/4 cup powdered sugar

1/2 cup unsalted butter, melted

For the Lemon Filling:

6 lemons, zest and juice

4 eggs

1 1/4 cups sugar

2 tablespoons all purpose flour

1/2 teaspoon kosher salt

1/2 teaspoon vanilla extract

Method:

1. *Preheat oven to 350°F.*

2. *In a bowl, stir all crust ingredients together until a crumbly dough forms.*

3. *Press the dough into the bottom of an 8 x 8-inch or 9 x 9-inch pan.*

4. *Bake for 15-20 minutes or until light golden brown; remove and set aside.*

5. *Use the **FINE GRATER** or **CITRUS ZESTER** to zest the lemons until you have 2 tablespoons zest; transfer to a bowl.*

6. *Use the **BIRDS BEAK GARNISHING KNIFE** to cut lemons in half then squeeze 1/2 cup of juice into the bowl.*

7. *Add remaining filling ingredients to the bowl; whisk until smooth.*

8. *Pour filling over the hot crust.*

9. *Return to the oven and bake for 20-25 minutes or until filling is set (do not over bake).*

10. *Let cool to room temperature, garnish as desired and serve.*

BABY SHOWER
BABY CARRIAGE

Makes 10-15 servings

Ingredients:

1 large watermelon, seedless
1 honeydew melon
1 cantaloupe
1 bunch red grapes
1 bunch green grapes
1 ruby red grapefruit
1 orange

Method:

1. *Use a large knife to cut the bottom off of the watermelon so it sits flat.*
2. *To remove the carriage top, use the **V-SHAPED CUTTER** to cut out the top portion then use the **BIRDS BEAK GARNISHING KNIFE** to cut around the sides (A).*
3. *Use the **DUAL MELON BALLER** to scoop melon balls from the melons and cantaloupe; set aside.*
4. *Use the **BIRDS BEAK GARNISHING KNIFE** to cut small slices from the grapes to create the eyes (B).*
5. *Use 3 cantaloupe balls to create the ears and nose (B).*
6. *Use the **BIRDS BEAK GARNISHING KNIFE** to cut a hole into the grapefruit big enough to hold the pacifier.*
7. *Attach the face components to the grapefruit using small pieces of bamboo skewer.*
8. *Use the **BIRDS BEAK GARNISHING KNIFE** to cut 4 wheels from the orange.*
9. *Attach orange wheels to the watermelon using pieces of bamboo skewer; add honeydew balls as hubcaps (C).*
10. *Place the grapefruit baby into the carriage then add the melon balls and grapes (D).*
11. *Arrange any extra melon balls or grapes around the carriage before serving.*

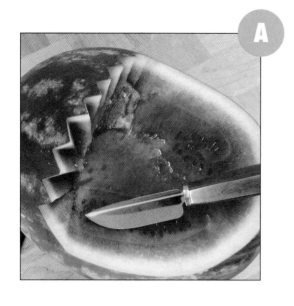

EASTER BUNNY
BASKET

Makes 4-6 servings

Ingredients:

1 large honeydew melon
1 wedge seedless watermelon
1/2 cantaloupe
1 pint blueberries
1 carrot
1/2 cup red grapes
2 limes

Method:

1. *Trim a small slice off the honeydew melon bottom so it sits flat.*

2. *Use a bamboo skewer to outline the bunny pattern (A).*

3. *Use the **BIRDS BEAK GARNISHING KNIFE** to cut out the bunny pattern (B).*

4. *Use the **DUAL MELON BALLER** to scoop balls from the honeydew melon, watermelon and cantaloupe.*

5. *For the bunny's eyes, use small pieces of bamboo skewer to attach 2 blueberries to the front of the bunny's face.*

6. *Use the **Y-PEELER** to peel the carrot then use the **BIRDS BEAK GARNISHING KNIFE** to cut the carrot into long whiskers.*

7. *Secure the whiskers to the bunny's face using additional bamboo skewer pieces (C).*

8. *Use the **STAINLESS STEEL CHOPPER** to scoop and transfer the melon balls and grapes into the bunny's body.*

9. *Use the **BIRDS BEAK GARNISHING KNIFE** to slice the limes into thin wheels and arrange around the bunny before serving.*

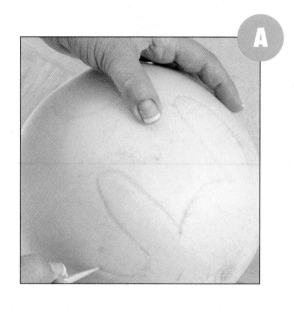

A

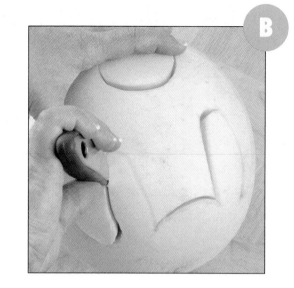

B

C

PINEAPPLE DESSERT
WEDGES

Makes 4 servings

Ingredients:

1 large ripe pineapple
1 lime, zest and juice
3 tablespoons sugar
1 piece fresh coconut
A few sprigs fresh mint

Method:

1. *Use a large knife to quarter the pineapple lengthwise, leaving the crown on (A).*
2. *Use the **BIRDS BEAK GARNISHING KNIFE** to separate the flesh from the rind (B).*
3. *Use the **BIRDS BEAK GARNISHING KNIFE** to remove the core.*
4. *Use the **BIRDS BEAK GARNISHING KNIFE** to carve 2 decorative notches down the length of each side (C).*
5. *Use the **CRINKLE CUTTER** to slice each wedge vertically to create individual slices (D).*
6. *Use the **CITRUS ZESTER** to zest the lime into a small bowl.*
7. *Use the **BIRDS BEAK GARNISHING KNIFE** to cut lime in half then squeeze the juice over the zest then stir in the sugar.*
8. *Drizzle sugar mixture over the pineapple wedges.*
9. *Place on individual plates then grate coconut over the pineapple using the **FINE GRATER**.*
10. *Use the **KITCHEN SHEARS** to snip some mint for garnish before serving.*

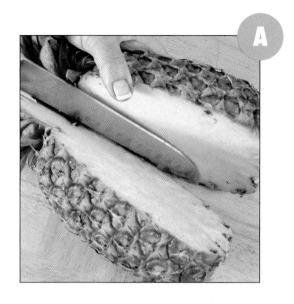

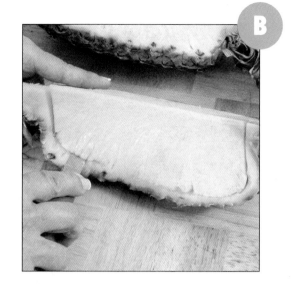

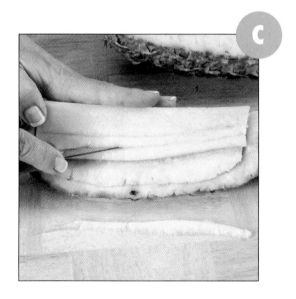

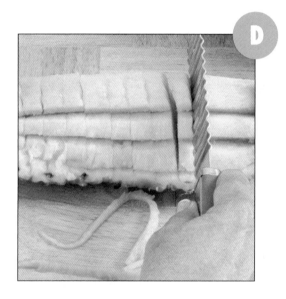

SCHOOL BUS

Makes 6-8 servings

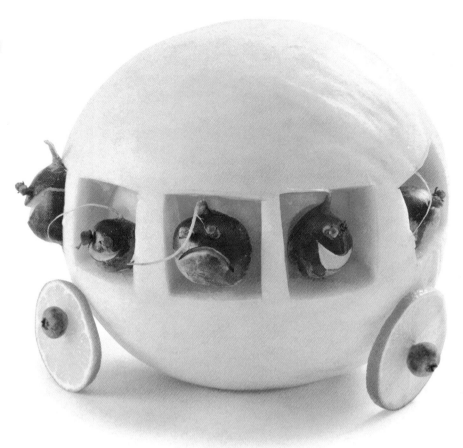

Ingredients:

1 honeydew melon
1 bunch radishes
12 whole cloves
1 small lime
1 pint blueberries
1 pint strawberries
1 pint raspberries
1/4 cup granulated sugar
1/4 cup water
1 teaspoon lemon juice
1/4 teaspoon vanilla extract

Method:

1. *Use a large knife to cut the bottom off the honeydew melon so it sits flat.*
2. *Use the **BIRDS BEAK GARNISHING KNIFE** to create windows by carving out four 1/2-inch deep squares on the side of the melon (A).*
3. *Use the **DUAL MELON BALLER** to scoop out the flesh in each window to hold the radishes (B).*
4. *Use the **V-SHAPED CUTTER** to cut an opening on the other side of the honeydew melon (C).*
5. *Reserve all the flesh then use the **DUAL MELON BALLER** to scoop balls from flesh; set aside.*
6. *Select radishes then cut out the mouths using the **BIRDS BEAK GARNISHING KNIFE** (D).*
7. *Stick two cloves into each of the radishes to make the eyes (E).*
8. *Attach radish heads to the windows of the school bus using pieces of bamboo skewer (F).*
9. *Use the **BIRDS BEAK GARNISHING KNIFE** to slice 4 wheels from the lime.*
10. *Attach wheels to the sides of the bus using pieces of bamboo skewer; use blueberries for the hubcaps.*
11. *Fill the back of the school bus with the melon balls and remaining fruit.*
12. *Combine the sugar, water, lemon juice and vanilla in a spray bottle.*
13. *Spray the fruit with sugar mixture before serving.*

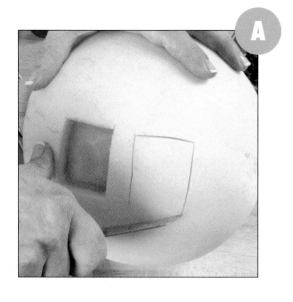

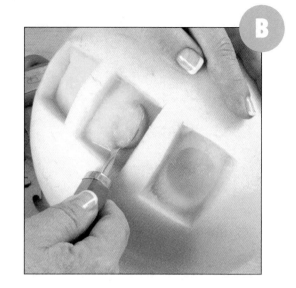

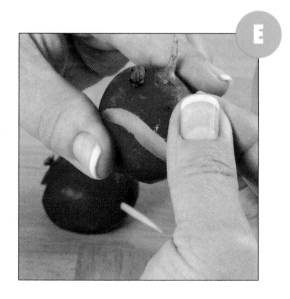

THANKSGIVING
FRUIT BASKET

Makes 12-15 servings

Ingredients:

1 large watermelon, seedless
1 honeydew melon
1 cantaloupe
3 kiwi
1 package fresh blueberries
1/3 cup granulated sugar
1/4 cup apple juice
1 teaspoon lemon juice
1/2 teaspoon vanilla extract

Method:

1. *Use a large knife to cut the bottom off the watermelon so it sits flat (A).*
2. *Draw a turkey on a piece paper to make a template; cut it out using the **KITCHEN SHEARS**.*
3. *Attach the turkey template to the side of the watermelon using tape.*
4. *Trace the turkey outline on the side of the watermelon using a bamboo skewer (B) then deepen the lines using the **BIRDS BEAK GARNISHING KNIFE** (C).*
5. *Use the **BIRDS BEAK GARNISHING KNIFE** to remove the flesh around the turkey shape (D).*
6. *Use the **V-SHAPED CUTTER** to cut an oval opening into the top of the watermelon; reserve usable flesh (E).*
7. *Use the **DUAL MELON BALLER** to scoop balls from the melons and cantaloupe (F).*
8. *Use the **BIRDS BEAK GARNISHING KNIFE** to peel the kiwi then slice them using the **CRINKLE CUTTER**.*
9. *Use a maple leaf-shaped cookie cutter to cut out shapes from the melons then place on long bamboo skewers.*
10. *Fill the basket with melon balls, kiwi and blueberries then add the skewered maple leaves.*
11. *In a small bowl, stir together remaining ingredients.*
12. *Pour mixture into a spray bottle then spray the fruit before serving.*

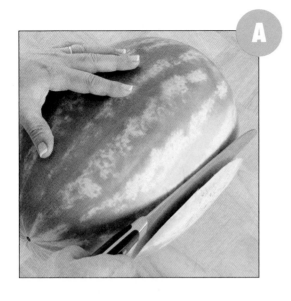

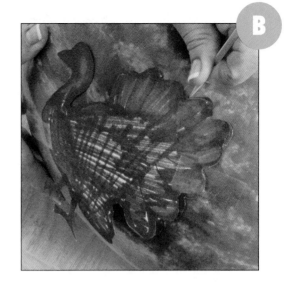

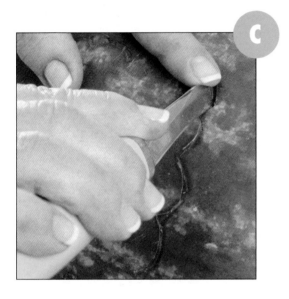

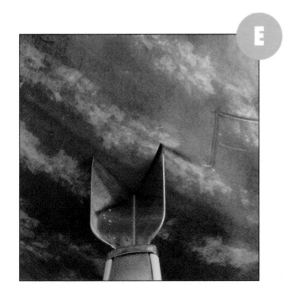

100% FRUIT WEDDING CAKE

Makes 10-15 servings

Ingredients:

2 medium watermelons, seedless
2 pints blueberries

Method:

1. *Use a large knife to cut both watermelons in half vertically.*

2. *Use a large knife to trim off all the rind from the watermelons (A).*

3. *Cut a 4-inch thick bottom tier from 1 watermelon half by using a glass bowl as a guide to so that the watermelon tier has round sides (B).*

4. *Use the **CRINKLE CUTTER** to trim another 4-inch thick tier; use a smaller glass bowl as a guide to cut this tier 2 inches less in diameter than the first one (C).*

5. *Use the **BIRDS BEAK GARNISHING KNIFE** to trim another 4-inch thick tier; use a smaller coffee cup as a guide to cut this tier 2 inches less in diameter than the second tier (D).*

6. *Place the first tier on a cake pedestal then top with the second and third tier.*

7. *Arrange the blueberries around each tier like a border (E).*

8. *Use a small heart-shaped cookie cutter to cut a heart from the remaining watermelon.*

9. *Place heart on a long bamboo skewer then push into the top tier before serving (F).*

ST. PATRICK'S DAY
FRUIT BASKET

Makes 6-8 servings

Ingredients:

1 honeydew melon
1 cantaloupe
3 kiwi
1 bunch green grapes
1/3 cup granulated sugar
1/4 cup apple juice
1 teaspoon lemon juice
1/2 teaspoon vanilla extract

Method:

1. *Use a large knife to cut the bottom off the honeydew melon so it sits flat.*
2. *Use a shamrock-shaped cookie cutter and a meat mallet to tap shamrocks onto the side of the melon (A).*
3. *Use the **BIRDS BEAK GARNISHING KNIFE** to remove the flesh around the shamrocks (B).*
4. *Use the **V-SHAPED CUTTER** to cut a round opening into the top of the honeydew melon; reserve usable flesh (C).*
5. *Use the **DUAL MELON BALLER** to scoop balls from the honeydew melon and cantaloupe.*
6. *Use the **BIRDS BEAK GARNISHING KNIFE** to peel the kiwi then slice them using the **CRINKLE CUTTER**.*
7. *Use the shamrock-shaped cookie cutter to cut out shapes from the melons then place on long bamboo skewers.*
8. *Fill the basket with melon balls, grapes and kiwi then add the skewered shamrocks.*
9. *In a small bowl, stir together remaining ingredients.*
10. *Pour mixture into a spray bottle then spray the fruit before serving.*

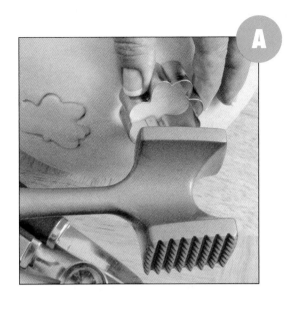

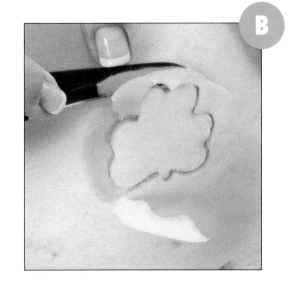

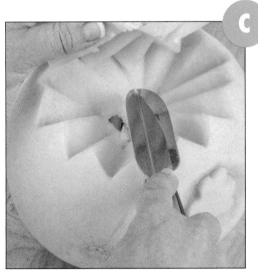

VALENTINE'S DAY
FRUIT BASKET

Makes 4-6 servings

Ingredients:

1 watermelon, seedless
1 honeydew melon
1 cantaloupe
1/3 cup granulated sugar
1/4 cup apple juice
1 teaspoon lemon juice
1/2 teaspoon vanilla extract

Method:

1. *Use a large knife to cut the bottom off the watermelon so it sits flat.*
2. *Use a heart-shaped cookie cutter and a mallet to tap hearts into the side of the watermelon, making sure to go through the rind of the watermelon (A).*
3. *Use the **BIRDS BEAK GARNISHING KNIFE** to remove the flesh around the heart shapes (B).*
4. *Use the **V-SHAPED CUTTER** to cut an oval opening into the top of the watermelon; reserve usable flesh (C).*
5. *Use the **DUAL MELON BALLER** to scoop balls from the melons and cantaloupe.*
6. *Use the heart-shaped cookie cutters to cut out shapes from the melons then place on long bamboo skewers (D).*
7. *Fill the basket with melon balls then add the skewered hearts.*
8. *In a small bowl, stir together remaining ingredients.*
9. *Pour mixture into a spray bottle then spray the fruit before serving.*

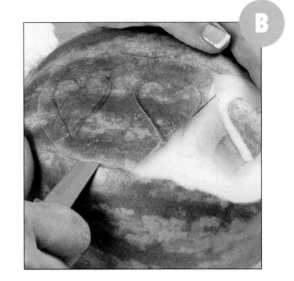

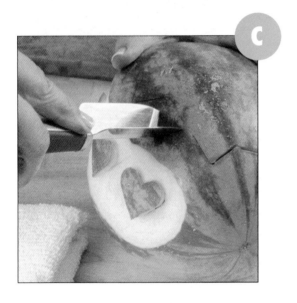

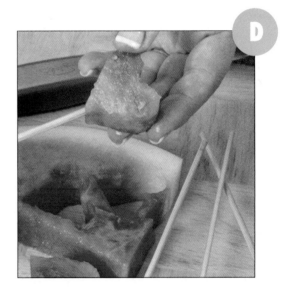

WEDDING SHOWER

FRUIT BOWL

Makes 6-8 servings

Ingredients:

1 watermelon, seedless
1 honeydew melon
1 cantaloupe
3 oranges
4 whole cloves
Piece of cheesecloth
Black construction paper and glue
1 bunch red grapes
1 pint blueberries

Method:

1. *Use a large knife to cut the bottom off the watermelon so it sits flat.*
2. *Use a bamboo skewer to trace the car opening into the top of the watermelon.*
3. *Use the **BIRDS BEAK GARNISHING KNIFE** to cut out the car opening; reserve the rind and usable flesh (A).*
4. *Use the **BIRDS BEAK GARNISHING KNIFE** to cut a rectangular windshield from the reserved rind (B) then add decorative edges using the **CHANNEL KNIFE** (C).*
5. *Use the **DUAL MELON BALLER** to scoop balls from the melons and cantaloupe; set aside.*
6. *Use the **BIRDS BEAK GARNISHING KNIFE** to slice 4 wheels from an orange.*
7. *Attach the wheels to the sides of the watermelon using pieces of bamboo skewer then use melon balls for hubcaps (D).*
8. *Attach "headlights" to the front of the melon using melon balls and pieces of bamboo skewer.*
9. *Use the stem end of each of the remaining oranges as the mouths then attached two cloves to each orange to make the eyes (E).*
10. *Use the **KITCHEN SHEARS** to cut out a piece of cheesecloth for a veil then use it to cut a hat from the construction paper; glue the hat together.*
11. *Attach the veil and hat to the oranges using pieces of bamboo skewers; use blueberries to create a tiara by attaching to the bamboo skewers holding the veil.*
12. *Attach the windshield to the melon using pieces of bamboo skewer then position the bride and groom behind the windshield (F).*
13. *Fill the car with melon balls, grapes and blueberries before serving.*

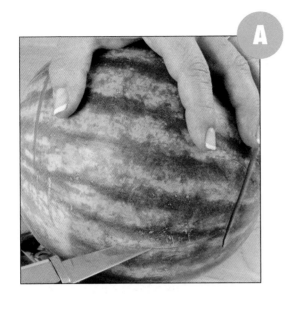

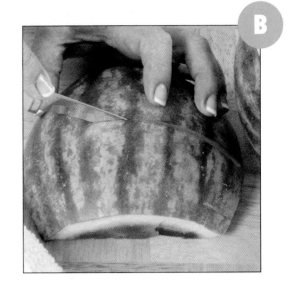

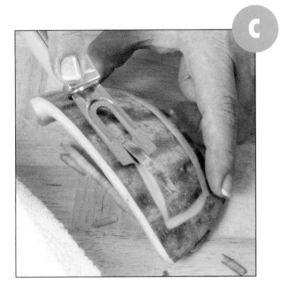

100% FRUIT
BIRTHDAY CAKE

Makes 8-10 servings

Ingredients:

1 medium watermelon, seedless
2 kiwi
1/2 of a cantaloupe
1/2 honeydew melon
1 cup blueberries

Method:

1. *Use a large knife to trim the top and bottom from the watermelon so it sits flat and has a flat surface.*

2. *Use the **CRINKLE CUTTER** to trim the sides using a glass bowl as a guide so that the watermelon has round sides (A).*

3. *Use the **BIRDS BEAK GARNISHING KNIFE** to peel the kiwi.*

4. *Use the **CRINKLE CUTTER** to slice the kiwi then attach to the sides using pieces of bamboo skewer (B).*

5. *Use the **DUAL MELON BALLER** to scoop balls from the cantaloupe and honeydew then arrange around the base of the watermelon like a border (C).*

6. *Use a flower-shaped cookie cutter to cut a flower out of the honeydew melon and place on top of the watermelon.*

7. *Use the **DUAL MELON BALLER** to scoop a divot out of the center of the flower then add a cantaloupe melon ball (D & E).*

8. *Use a heart-shaped cookie cutter and cut hearts from the cantaloupe then attach to the sides of the watermelon using pieces of bamboo skewer (F).*

9. *Arrange the blueberries around the top edge to form a top border.*

10. *Add birthday candles if desired before serving.*

HONEYDEW MELON
FLOWER

Makes 4-6 servings

Ingredients:

1 honeydew melon
1 watermelon wedge, seedless

Method:

1. *Use a large knife to cut the bottom off the honeydew melon so it sits flat.*
2. *Use the **BIRDS BEAK GARNISHING KNIFE** to cut out v-shaped flower petals from the honeydew melon (A) then remove the top half (B).*
3. *Use the **BIRDS BEAK GARNISHING KNIFE** to cut notches into each petal (C).*
4. *Use the **BIRDS BEAK GARNISHING KNIFE** to cut down each of the petals twice to separate the flesh from the rind and to open up the petals (D & E).*
5. *Use the **DUAL MELON BALLER** to scoop balls from the watermelon wedge.*
6. *Use the **STAINLESS STEEL CHOPPER** to gather up the balls then place them in the center of the honeydew flower (F).*
7. *Garnish as desired and serve.*

FOURTH OF JULY
FRUIT BOWL

Makes 12-15 servings

Ingredients:

1 large watermelon, seedless
1 honeydew melon
1 cantaloupe
3 kiwi
1 package fresh blueberries

Method:

1. *Use a large knife to cut the bottom off the watermelon so it sits flat.*
2. *Use the **CHANNEL KNIFE** to cut the flag's outline and stripes into the side of the watermelon (A & B).*
3. *Use the **CITRUS ZESTER** to create the stars (B & C).*
4. *Use a star-shaped cookie cutter and a meat mallet to tap a star on each side of the flag.*
5. *Use the **BIRDS BEAK GARNISHING KNIFE** to remove the flesh around the stars.*
6. *Use a bamboo skewer to outline the basket handle on top of the watermelon (D).*
7. *Use the **V-SHAPED CUTTER** to cut out the basket area, reserving usable flesh (E).*
8. *Use the **DUAL MELON BALLER** to scoop balls from the melons and cantaloupe.*
9. *Use a star-shaped cookie cutter to cut out stars from the melons and cantaloupe (F).*
10. *Place the stars on long bamboo skewers.*
11. *Use the **BIRDS BEAK GARNISHING KNIFE** to peel the kiwi then slice them using the **CRINKLE CUTTER**.*
12. *Fill the basket with melon balls, kiwi and blueberries then add the skewered stars.*
13. *Arrange some additional melon balls around the watermelon to make a decorative border before serving.*

TIP

For an extra touch, you can use a small brush or cotton swab to paint red food coloring on the stripes of the flag and blue food coloring on the stars area.

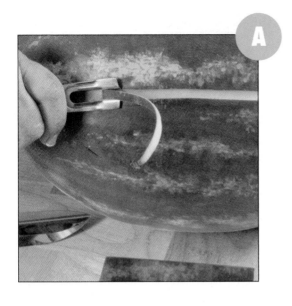

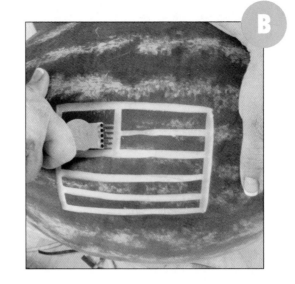

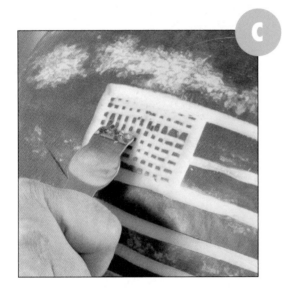

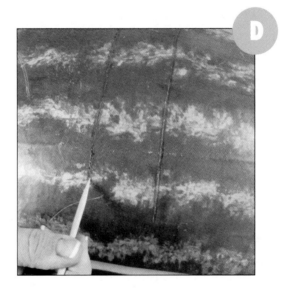

PRETTY PINEAPPLE
BOATS

Makes 4 servings

Ingredients:

1 ripe pineapple with crown
1/2 honeydew melon
1 kiwi
1/4 cup granulated sugar
1/4 cup water
1 teaspoon lemon juice
1/4 teaspoon vanilla extract

Method:

1. *Use the **CRINKLE CUTTER** to trim the pineapple crown (A).*
2. *Use the **V-SHAPED CUTTER** to cut around the pineapple at a 45° angle (B).*
3. *Remove the pineapple flesh using the **BIRDS BEAK GARNISHING KNIFE,** leaving a 1/2-inch thick shell (C).*
4. *Rinse out the pineapple shell if any of the brown rind remains.*
5. *Use the **DUAL MELON BALLER** to scoop balls from the honeydew melon.*
6. *Fill the boat with honeydew balls.*
7. *Use the **V-SHAPED CUTTER** to cut kiwi in half then place around the pineapple (D).*
8. *In a bowl whisk together the sugar, water, lemon and vanilla.*
9. *Drizzle sugar mixture over the fruit before serving.*

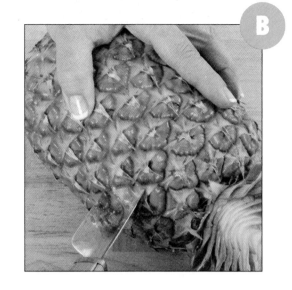

GRADUATION FRUIT BASKET

Makes 10-15 servings

Ingredients:

1 large watermelon, seedless
1 honeydew melon
1 cantaloupe
1 pineapple
1 pint blueberries
1 bunch green grapes
1 pint strawberries
2 cups chocolate chips
1 cup white chocolate chips
1/3 cup coconut oil

Method:

1. *Use a large knife to cut the bottom off the watermelon so it sits flat.*
2. *Use the **V-SHAPED CUTTER** to cut an opening into the top of the watermelon; reserve lid (A).*
3. *Use the **APPLE CORER** to punch a hole border around the watermelon (B).*
4. *Use a large knife to slice the rind off one side of the watermelon (C).*
5. *Using alphabet cookie cutters, cut desired letters from the watermelon flesh of the removed lid then attach to the side of the watermelon using small pieces of bamboo skewer (D).*
6. *Use the **DUAL MELON BALLER** to scoop balls from the melons and cantaloupe.*
7. *Use the **BIRDS BEAK GARNISHING KNIFE** to trim and peel the pineapple.*
8. *Use the **APPLE CORER** to remove the pineapple core then cut pineapple into pieces using the **CRINKLE CUTTER**.*
9. *Fill the basket with melon balls, pineapple, blueberries and grapes.*
10. *Place the strawberries on long bamboo skewers.*
11. *Place each color chocolate chips into a separate microwave-safe bowl.*
12. *Divide the coconut oil between the bowls then microwave each for 30 seconds.*
13. *Stir and repeat until fluid.*
14. *Dip skewered strawberries into either color chocolate then drizzle with other chocolate to make a pretty design if desired before adding to the basket (E).*

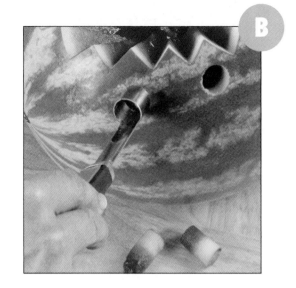

BIRTHDAY
FRUIT BOWL

Makes 12-15 servings

Ingredients:

1 large watermelon, seedless
1 honeydew melon
1 cantaloupe
1 pint raspberries
1 pint blueberries
1 pint strawberries
3 cups chocolate chips
1/2 cup coconut oil
Large marshmallows

Method:

1. *Use a large knife to cut the bottom off the watermelon so it sits flat.*
2. *Use the **V-SHAPED CUTTER** to cut a large opening into the top of the watermelon; reserve usable flesh (A).*
3. *To add a name or message to the watermelon, trace letters into the rind of the watermelon using a bamboo skewer (B).*
4. *Use the **BIRDS BEAK GARNISHING KNIFE** to remove the flesh around the letters (C).*
5. *Use the **DUAL MELON BALLER** to scoop balls from the melons and cantaloupe (D).*
6. *Use the **STAINLESS STEEL CHOPPER** to scoop and transfer the melon balls to the watermelon basket then add the raspberries, blueberries and some strawberries; arrange some extra melon balls around the watermelon if desired.*
7. *In a microwave-safe bowl, combine the chocolate chips and coconut oil.*
8. *Microwave for 1 minute then stir and repeat until chocolate is fluid.*
9. *Place marshmallows and strawberries on long bamboo skewers then dip into the fluid chocolate before placing them in the fruit basket.*
10. *Add long birthday candles if desired before serving.*

104

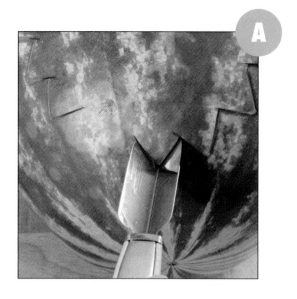

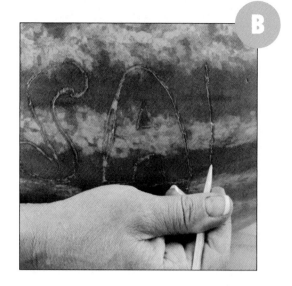

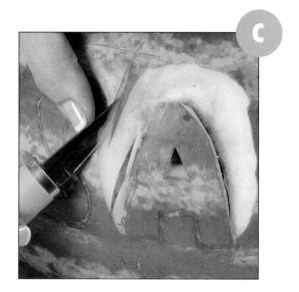

TIP

To add a pop of color, use food coloring to color the name or message on the watermelon.

SOURCE PAGE

Here are some of my favorite places to find ingredients that are not readily available at grocery stores as well as kitchen tools and supplies that help you become a better cook.

The Bakers Catalogue at King Arthur Flour

135 Route 5 South
P.O. Box 1010
Norwich, VT 05055

Pure fruit oils, citric acid, silicone spatulas, digital timers, oven thermometers, real truffle oil, off-set spatulas, measuring cups and spoons, knives, ice cream scoops, cheesecloth, cookie sheets, baking pans
www.kingarthurflour.com

Chocosphere

P.O. Box 2237
Tualatin, OR 97062
877-992-4623

Excellent quality cocoa (Callebaut)
All Chocolates
Jimmies and sprinkles
www.chocosphere.com

Gluten Free Mall

4927 Sonoma HWY Suite C1
Santa Rosa, CA 95409
707-509-4528

All ingredients needed for gluten-free baking
www.glutenfreemall.com

D & G Occasions

625 Herndon Ave.
Orlando, FL 32803
407-894-4458

My favorite butter vanilla extract by Magic Line, cake and candy making supplies, citric acid, pure fruit oils, professional food colorings, ultra thin flexible spatulas, large selection of sprinkles and jimmies, unusual birthday candles, pure vanilla extract, pastry bags and tips, parchment, off-set spatulas, oven and candy thermometers, kitchen timers, meat mallets, large selection of cookie cutters
www.dandgoccasions.com

Penzeys Spices

P.O. Box 924
Brookfield, WI 53045
800-741-7787

Spices, extracts, seasonings, seasonal cookie cutters, mallets and more
www.penzeys.com

INDEX